STUDY GUIDE • Lucia A. Worthington

INTERNATIONAL BUSINESS

Environments and Operations

NINTH EDITION

JOHN D.
DANIELS • RADEBAUGH
LEE H.

Acquisitions editor: David Shafer
Associate editor: Michele Foresta
Production editor: Leah Crescenzo
Manufacturer: Victor Graphics, Inc.

ISBN 0-13-018431-4

10 9 8 7 6 5 4 3 2 1

Table of Contents

Chapter 1 – International Business: An Overview 1

Chapter 2 – The Cultural Environments Facing Business 9

Chapter 3 – The Political and Legal Environments Facing Business 18

Chapter 4 – The Economic Environment...26

Chapter 5 – International Trade Theory..34

Chapter 6 – Governmental Influence on Trade...42

Chapter 7 – Regional Economic Integration and Cooperative Agreements 50

Chapter 8 – Foreign Direct Investment..59

Chapter 9 – The Foreign Exchange Market 68

Chapter 10 – The Determination of Exchange Rates..75

Chapter 11 – Governmental Attitudes toward Foreign Direct Investment 81

Chapter 12 – International Business Negotiation and Diplomacy...89

Chapter 13 – Country Evaluation and Selection...98

Chapter 14 – Collaborative Strategies 107

Chapter 15 – Control Strategies 115

Chapter 16 – Marketing 123

Chapter 17 – Export and Import Strategies..131

Chapter 18 – Global Manufacturing and Supply Chain Management....................................140

Chapter 19 – Multinational Accounting and Tax Functions..148

Chapter 20 – The Multinational Finance Function..156

Chapter 21 – Human Resource Management 164

Chapter 1

International Business: An Overview

CHAPTER OBJECTIVES

1. To define international business and describe how it differs from domestic business.

2. To explain why companies engage in international business and why its growth has accelerated.

3. To introduce different modes a company can use to accomplish its global objectives.

4. To illustrate the role social science disciplines play in understanding the environment of international business.

5. To provide an overview of the primary patterns for companies' international expansion.

6. To describe the major countervailing forces that affect international business.

TRUE/FALSE

1. International business includes all commercial transactions—among the private sector only—and between two or more countries. T/F

    Hint   Consider that governments are also big international customers.

2. Global events and competition generally affect only large companies. T/F

    Hint   Consider the complex interrelationships of international business.

3. A company's external environment becomes more diverse when it operates internationally. T/F

    Hint   Consider additional complexities such as geographic differences, political differences, and societal differences.

4. One major reason companies engage in international trade is to minimize sales. T/F

    Hint   Going beyond one's domestic regions offers expanded sales opportunities.

5. International business has been growing at a faster pace than domestic business has grown generally. T/F

    Hint   The portion of world output accounted for by foreign-owned facilities has been growing substantially.

6. Liberalization by governments has contributed to the increased growth in international business in the last decade. T/F

    Hint   Governments today impose fewer restrictions on cross-border movements than they did a decade or two ago.

7. Merchandise exports are intangible products—goods—sent out of a country. T/F

    Hint   Merchandise goods can be seen and felt.

8. Tourism and transportation are considered service exports. T/F

   Hint   When new money is brought into a home country for a service, then the service is considered an export.

9. A foreign direct investment (FDI) gives the investor a controlling interest in a foreign company. T/F

   Hint   Control need not be at 100% or even a 50% interest.

10. A multidomestic company is also called a locally responsive company. T/F

    Hint   A multidomestic company allows each of its foreign-country operations to act fairly independently within its host country.

11. Political leaders control whether and how international business takes place. T/F

    Hint   Consider how the conflict between Cuba and the United States has shaped trade between these two countries.

12. A knowledge of geography is superfluous to international trade. T/F

    Hint   Geography is the key to understanding barriers, climate, communications systems, the probability of natural disasters, climate conditions, and so on.

13. The different competitive strategies between Volkswagen and Rolls-Royce explains why Rolls Royce is not overly concerned with low labor costs. T/F

    Hint   Volkswagen sells to a price-conscious clientele while Rolls-Royce sells a luxury car where prices tend not to matter.

14. Exporting tends to require the least commitment and risk at the early stages of a company's international involvement. T/F

    Hint   Refer to Figure 1.7 which shows a progression of activities as companies become international.

15. Carlsberg, a Danish brewery, gave in to consumer pressure to drop out of a joint venture in a country with a military dictatorship. T/F

    Hint   Carlsberg decided that union and customer lobbies at home would determine its domestic market and gave in to pressure to drop a joint venture in Myanmar.

MULTIPLE CHOICE

1. What are the four major operating objectives that may influence companies to engage in international business?

   Hint   Consider competition, survival, and growth factors.

   a.   The four major operating objectives that may influence companies to engage in international business are to help the economies of developing countries, liaison with their preferred ethnic groups, maximize competitive risks, and acquire resources.
   b.   To minimize domestic sales, acquire resources, diversify sales, and minimize competitive risks.
   c.   To expand sales, acquire resources, diversify sources of sales and supplies, and minimize competitive risks.
   d.   None of the above

2

2. The rapid increase in and expansion of technology has increased growth in international trade mainly because:

   Hint   Consider transportation factors and telecommunications.

   a. carrier pigeons have become extinct.
   b. governments have become increasingly protectionist.
   c. global competition is less severe, and therefore it is less risky to enter the international markets.
   d. there are four factors which include: rapid increase and expansion of technology and transportation, liberalization of government trade policies, development of institutions to support international trade, and the necessity to counter increased global competition.

3. Support services to ease international business transactions include:

   Hint   Consider the processes needed to ship goods and complete payment transactions.

   a. banking services that include currency conversions, letters of credit, and collections.
   b. postal services facilitated by national governments and private couriers.
   c. advanced transportation systems.
   d. all of the above.

4. Collaborative arrangements describe the numerous ways companies can work together, and they include:

   Hint   Consider long-term and short-term relationships.

   a. licensing.
   b. management contracts.
   c. branch office arrangements.
   d. both (a) and (b).

5. Multinational enterprise (MNE) and multinational corporation (MNC) tend to mean the same thing.

   Hint   Enterprise is a generic term, whereas corporation connotes a legal entity.

   a. MNE refers to start-up operations only.
   b. The term MNC is used only for very large international corporations.
   c. Yes, the terms MNE and MNC are used interchangeably.
   d. MNEs are found only in command economies, and MNCs are found only in free enterprise systems.

6. Lucasfilm cannot distribute "The Phantom Menace" in Cuba because:

   Hint   Consider the political relations between Cuba and the United States.

   a. the Cubans speak Spanish, not English.
   b. the United States forbids U.S. exports to Cuba.
   c. Cubans boycott science fiction films.
   d. Cuban labor unions will object to importing foreign films.

7. Intermediaries are commonly used by companies during the first stages of international expansion because:

   Hint   Intermediaries are professional trade experts.

   a. intermediaries are very difficult to find and are rarely used.
   b. intermediaries are found only outside of the company's home country and therefore are too expensive and unreliable.
   c. intermediaries, once used, demand a lifetime contractual relationship with their customers.
   d. intermediaries are an excellent way to begin international trade transactions.

8. When companies first move internally, they are apt to tend to:

Hint Refer to Figure 1.7, axis D.

a. trade with their closest neighbor.
b. trade with the wealthiest countries.
c. trade with developing countries.
d. select one or a very few countries initially.

9. Any company operating internationally must:

Hint Consider the countervailing forces in international business.

a. standardize its product line.
b. use home country standards if the home country has a superior product.
c. consider host country factors in addition to company strategy.
d. always cater to the host country needs and adjust home country standards accordingly.

10. A company engaged in national responsiveness would:

Hint Consider what measures a company would need to take to serve a specific market outside of its home market.

a. avoid make operating adjustments where it does business to reach a satisfactory level of performance.
b. use a multidomestic approach.
c. practice a global strategy by standardizing its product line.
d. both (a) and (c) are correct.

11. Countries enter into treaties and agreements with other countries to:

Hint Treaties are either bilateral—between two countries, or multilateral—between more than two countries and seek to establish mutually beneficial relationships.

a. allow others' ships or planes to use certain seaports and airports.
b. establish domestic laws.
c. destroy infrastructure and telecommunications systems.
d. both (a) and (c) are correct.

INTERNET EXERCISES

Exercise 1
Michelin
http://www.michelin.com
Note their global presence. Where is Michelin located? What are its products? What is the Michelin employee profile? What type of a company is Michelin with regard to international business? Is it a multidomestic company, a global company, or a transnational company? Describe and be specific, and support your descriptions.

Exercise 2
Gillette Company
http://www.gillette.com/investors/bus_op_struct.html
Note their organizational structure and product line. Why do you think Gillette has this organizational structure? Would this structure be appropriate for a company such as Disney? Why or why not?

Exercise 3
World Trade Organization
http://www.wto.org
Familiarize yourself with the trade topics section and the "front page" news. What role does the WTO play in the liberalization of cross-border movements? Which countries are on the news front? How do you interpret the WTO role after visiting and familiarizing yourself with their web site?

Exercise 4
Disney
http://www.disney-asia.com
Explore the international sites. How many regional sites are there? What is Disney promoting at each site? Consider products as well as services. How is Disney promoting these sites to different national and language groups?

Exercise 5
Lucasfilm
http://www.lucasfilm.com/history.html
http://www.starwars.com
Consider the appeal of products to various international groups. Reread the introduction to Chapter 1 that discusses Lucasfilm within the international arena. How has the Lucasfilm international activity changed in the last 25 years? What have been the driving forces for this change?

Exercise 6
Discuss the relationship between national sovereignty and practices such as child labor, bribery, and or the use of pesticides which may be seen as acceptable in one country but illegal in another. What are the consequences of accepting practices in the host country which are illegal in one's home country?

CHAPTER 1 ANSWER KEY

True/False

1. False   The private sector undertakes transactions for profit, and governments may or may not be profit-motivated.
   Difficulty: moderate
   Topic: Introduction to the Field of International Business (IB)

2. False   Selling output and securing supplies from foreign countries are activities any size company undertakes.
   Difficulty: hard
   Topic: Introduction to the Field of International Business (IB)

3. True   Refer to Figure 1.2, and note the external influences which add to the complexities for companies trading internationally.
   Difficulty: easy
   Topic: External Influences on International Business

4. False   It is false to think that a company would undertake the complexities of international trade to reduce its sales potential.
   Difficulty: easy
   Topic: Why Companies Engage in International Business

5. True   According to the World Trade Organization, international business has been growing at a faster pace than it did earlier.
   Difficulty: moderate
   Topic: Reasons for Recent International Business Growth—From Carrier Pigeons to the Internet

6. True   Fewer restrictions enable companies to take better advantage of international opportunities.
   Difficulty: hard
   Topic: Liberalization of Cross-Border Movements

7. False   Merchandise exports are tangible because they are visible and can be seen and felt.
   Difficulty: moderate
   Topic: Merchandise Exports and Imports

8. True   When tourists visit a country, that country sells services to foreigners; this is considered a form of export.
   Difficulty: hard
   Topic: Tourism and Transportation

9. True   An FDI represents an interest in a foreign investment
   Difficulty: moderate
   Topic: Direct Investment

10. True   A multidomestic company may produce goods specifically for a French market in France and produce a similar good to suit Japanese tastes in the Japanese market.
    Difficulty: moderate
    Topic: International Companies and Terms to Describe Them

11. True   Political disputes can disrupt trade and investments. It is therefore imperative that political risks are identified before trade agreements are made.
    Difficulty: moderate
    Topic: Understanding a Company's Physical and Societal Environments

12. False   It is important to know geography because it identifies transportation routes, market needs because of climate, terrain, etc.
    Difficulty: hard
    Topic: Understanding a Company's Physical and Societal Environments

13. True   Volkswagen's competitive strategy requires this company to seek low labor production costs.
    Difficulty: moderate
    Topic: Competitive Environment

14. True   Exporting as well as importing is a good way to test international markets, and these methods minimize risks at the introduction stage.
    Difficulty: easy
    Topic: Evolution of Strategy in the Internalization Process

15. True   Although Carlsberg did not see itself as a foreign policy decision maker, the company minimized its risks from domestic boycotts by conceding the joint venture abroad.
    Difficulty: hard
    Topic: Ethical Dilemmas and Social Responsibilities

Multiple Choice

1. c.   These are the four major operating objectives. Refer to Figure 1.2 to view how these objectives fit with company strategy.
    Difficulty: moderate
    Topic: Why Companies Engage in International Business

2. d.   All four factors mentioned have had an impact on the expansion of international trade.
    Difficulty: hard
    Topic: Reasons for Recent International Business Growth—From Carrier Pigeons to the Internet

3. d.   (a), (b), and (c) are correct.
    Difficulty: moderate
    Topic: Reasons for Recent International Business Growth—From Carrier Pigeons to the Internet

4. d.   Licensing and management contracts are only some of the collaborative arrangements possible.
    Difficulty: moderate
    Topic: International Companies and Terms to Describe Them

5. c.   In addition to MNC and MNE, the United Nations also uses the word transnational company or TNC.
    Difficulty: hard
    Topic: International Companies and Terms to Describe Them

6. b.   The United States has had a trade embargo with Cuba since the 1960s.
    Difficulty: hard
    Topic: Understanding a Company's Physical and Societal Environment

7. d.   Most companies and individuals find the services of intermediaries helpful and necessary at the beginning of their trading activities.
    Difficulty: moderate
    Topic: Evolution of Strategy in the Internalization Process

8. d.   Companies tend to test their international outreach on one or a few carefully selected countries and the markets with those countries.
    Difficulty: hard
    Topic: Evolution of Strategy in the Internalization Process—Geographic Diversification

9. c.   Companies need to consider different national preferences as well as their own operational and strategic goals.
    Difficulty: hard
    Topic: Countervailing Forces—Globally Standardized versus Nationally Responsive Practices

10. b.   A multidomestic approach considers differences among country needs.
    Difficulty: moderate
    Topic: Countervailing forces—Globally Standardized versus Nationally Responsive Practices

11. a.   By establishing guidelines for using ports, countries can benefit from their use.
    Difficulty: moderate
    Topic: Sovereign versus Cross-National Relationships

Chapter 2

The Cultural Environments Facing Business

CHAPTER OBJECTIVES

1. To relate the problems and methods of learning about cultural environments.

2. To explain the major causes of cultural differences and change.

3. To examine behavioral factors influencing countries' business practices.

4. To examine cultural guidelines for companies that operate internationally.

TRUE/FALSE

1. The Parris-Rogers International (PRI) sales force found that there was less time to sell in the Middle East than in Europe. T/F

   Hint   Consider the Islamic prayer times and holy days.

2. Angela Clark adjusted to the Middle Eastern customs by wearing long-sleeved dresses in Saudi Arabia. T/F

   Hint   It is unlikely that a single businesswoman can obtain a visa to Saudi Arabia

3. Building cultural awareness can easily be learned by reading a book about that culture. T/F

   Hint   No simple foolproof methods exist to build cultural awareness.

4. There is general agreement that businesspeople can improve their awareness and sensitivity about other cultures. T/F

   Hint   Training programs based on research tend to enhance the likelihood of understanding other cultures.

5. National identity is perpetuated through rites and symbols of the country. T/F

   Hint   Symbols such as flags, national holidays, documents, and national monuments create a national identity.

6. Language plays an insignificant role in stabilizing a culture. T/F

   Hint   When people from different areas speak the same language, culture spreads easily.

7. McDonald's agreed not to serve beef in India because of a rumor that mad cow disease had contaminated the beef. T/F

   Hint   Hinduism considers the cow sacred.

8. Violence among religious groups is not a deterrent for companies conducting business internationally. T/F

   Hint   Religious wars or civil strife can affect political control and disrupt all aspects of conducting business.

9. The Protestant ethic, according to Max Weber, describes work as a means of salvation. T/F

   Hint   Max Weber observed that predominantly Protestant countries were the most economically developed.

10. In countries characterized by high risk avoidance, few consumers are prepared to take the social risk of trying a new product first. T/F

    Hint   It may be advantageous for a company to enter low risk avoidance markets such as Denmark and the United Kingdom rather than Belgium and Portugal which are high risk avoidance cultures.

11. High-context cultures spend little time on "small talk." T/F

    Hint   High-context cultures may consider trivial information important to understanding the complete picture.

12. Ethnocentrism is the belief that one's culture is superior to others. T/F

    Hint   In international business, an ethnocentric individual has the belief that what worked at home should work abroad.

13. Relativism holds that there are universal standards of behavior. T/F

    Hint   Relativism means something is relative to a particular group.

14. Government and academic leaders from many countries have criticized the Declaration of Human Rights for having too Western an orientation. T/F

    Hint   This Declaration was adopted by the United Nations in 1948.

15. Globalization of culture is illustrated by Japanese tourists listening to a Philippine group singing a U.S. song in an Indonesian hotel. T/F

    Hint   Contact across cultures is becoming more widespread than ever.

MULTIPLE CHOICE

1. The PRI case illustrates the problems that occur when:

   Hint   Consider the two distinct cultural approaches, one from the European perspective and the other from the Middle Eastern perspective.

   a.   different cultures often clash
   b.   English salesmen are geocentric.
   c.   a sales force does not possess a good work ethic.
   d.   both (a) and (c) are correct.

2. The British sales force in the PRI case considered chatting with customers over coffee:

   Hint   The British and the Arab business community had different concepts of what a business transaction entailed.

   a. a necessary part of conducting business.
   b. inappropriate because they preferred tea.
   c. a waste of time especially since they had "work to be done."
   d. both (a) and (c).

3. Culture is transmitted in various ways and includes:

   Hint   Culture is transmitted by those who have an influence on another person's behavior.

   a. cultural transmissions occur only between parent and child.
   b. cultural transmissions occur only between teacher and pupil.
   c. from parent to child, teacher to pupil, social leader to follower, and peer to peer.
   d. none of the above.

4. Affiliations determined by birth are:

   Hint   Consider that these affiliations are not choices the individual makes.

   a. known as ascribed group memberships and include those based on gender, family, age, caste, and ethnic, racial, or national origin.
   b. known as acquired groups.
   c. known as professional and political affiliations.
   d. none of the above.

5. Competence is of universal importance in establishing a person's eligibility for jobs.

   Hint   Culture dictates the criteria for job eligibility.

   a. Yes, the United States values competence for job eligibility, and the rest of the world follows this model.
   b. No, competence is not a major issue; seniority is of primary importance for job eligibility.
   c. No, a variety of factors determine job eligibility. The criteria are based in that country's value system and culture.
   d. All of the above.

6. Power distance describes the relationship between superiors and subordinates. Countries with high power distance include:

   Hint   High power distance tends to include an autocratic or paternalistic management style.

   a. Denmark and New Zealand.
   b. Malaysia and New Zealand,
   c. Austria and Denmark.
   d. none of the above.

7. Where collectivism is high, companies find their best marketing success when emphasizing:

   Hint   Consider that collectivism focuses on groups rather than the individual.

   a. individual needs.
   b. group values.
   c. all of the above.
   d. none of the above.

8. Monochronic cultures tend to:

   Hint   Consider that mono means one.

   a. prefer to work sequentially, such as finishing with one customer at a time.
   b. work on many tasks at once.
   c. consider peripheral information when making decisions.
   d. be fatalistic in nature.

9. The concept of silent language refers to:

   Hint   Consider the subtle forms of communication such as color, gestures, and distance.

   a. specifically, colors.
   b. specifically body language such as gestures, touching, walking.
   c. both time and space only.
   d. A collection of nonverbal cues that include: colors, distance used when communicating, perceptions and uses of time, and kinesics.

10. Culture shock occurs:

    Hint   Consider that culture shock happens when a person steps from one set of beliefs and assumptions into another setting.

    a. only when a person first enters a new country.
    b. when someone has not been briefed on a culture.
    c. when re-entering one's own country after a long absence.
    d. when one encounters frustration by having to learn and cope with a vast array of new cultural cues and expectations.

11. Ethnocentrism is the attitude that:

    Hint   Ethno is the root word that stands for race, culture, or people.

    a. cultural relativism is appropriate.
    b. there is only one god.
    c. one's own culture is superior to others.
    d. both (a) and (c) are correct.

12. Strategies for effectively instituting change in an international environment include:

    Hint   A series of methods that facilitate change and help reduce resistance to change.

    a. understanding the value system, good timing, and seeking the help of opinion leaders.
    b. making drastic changes quickly at the beginning to show leadership.
    c. mandating the change before people have a chance to resist.
    d. all of the above.

13. The normative approach to ethics holds that:

Hint   Consider the root word "norm" which means standard or universal.

   a.   ethical truths depend on the groups holding them and considers interventions unethical
   b.   "when in Rome, do as the Romans do."
   c.   there are universal standards that all cultures should follow.
   d.   the normative approach is not an ethical approach.

14. Situations that require making payments to government officials to secure contracts may be:

Hint   Consider host and home country laws and cultures

   a.   considered illegal in one country and legal in the other.
   b.   illegal in every country in the world.
   c.   considered illegal and unethical overall.
   d.   none of the above.

15. The John Higgins case is an example of a man who has a polycentric orientation.

Hint   Polycentrism is the behavior to adapt and adopt the host country culture.

   a.   Higgins is not polycentric. Instead, he is strongly ethnocentric.
   b.   No, Higgins is geocentric in his behavior.
   c.   There is not enough information in the case to consider if polycentric behavior is acted out.
   d.   Yes, Higgins clearly has transitioned to a polycentric style.

INTERNET EXERCISES

Exercise 1
Samsung
http://www.samsung.com
Explore the sections on culture, history, and religion. Consider how these cultural examples of Korea differ from your own. Visit at least five different areas including "Images and Sights of Korea." Write a brief overview of your impressions and how this relates to cultural awareness.
Difficulty: easy
Topic: The Nation as a Cultural Stabilizer

Exercise 2
Islamic religion and Hinduism
http://www.islam-qa.com/cgi-local/browse_home_eng
http://www.hinduismtoday.Kauai.hi.us
Explore each site to get a sense of each distinct religious tradition. Then, write a brief essay that discusses your findings including similarities and differences between them. How does this relate to the discussions on religions in this chapter? What can international companies learn from studying these two sites?
Difficulty: moderate
Topic: Religion and Culture as Stabilizer

Exercise 3
Arab net site
http://www.arab.net
Visit at least six links in the A-Z directory including Arabic cuisine and homes. How does the Arab culture differ from another culture that you know well? Do you see similarities? If so, what are they? Write a brief report of your findings to serve as a guide for company employees who will be working within the Arab communities. Establish some important guidelines for Arab cultural awareness.
Difficulty: moderate
Topic: Cultural Formation and Dynamism

Exercise 4
Arab net web site
http://www.arab.net
Compare the Saudi site with Bahrain and Morocco. What are the differences between these two sites? What are the similarities? What should an international manager know about these countries before conducting business in these countries? Write a brief set of guidelines outlining some of the highlights that you see as important to understanding these three Arab nations.
Difficulty: hard
Topic: The Nation as a Point of Reference

Exercise 5
Israeli site
http://www.ohr.org.il/web/study.htm
http://www.arab.net
Compare the Israeli site to two of its closest neighbors, Lebanon and Syria at www.arab.net. Note each country's dominant religion. What are they, and how significant is this religion in relation to that country's culture? You should be addressing Judaism, Christianity, and Islam in your analysis. What can an international company learn from your study? Discuss.
Difficulty: hard
Topic: Religion as a Cultural Stabilizer

CHAPTER 2 ANSWER KEY

True/False

1. True   The sales force had less time to sell because Muslims pray five times a day and also have considerably less time during the religious month of Ramadan.
   Difficulty: moderate
   Topic: Case: Parris-Rogers International

2. False   Angela Clark was not allowed to enter Saudi Arabia because she was a single woman. Furthermore, women in Saudi Arabia are obligated to wear the traditional abaya in public, and long-sleeved clothing would not have been enough in any event.
   Difficulty: moderate
   Topic: Case: Parris-Rogers International

3. False   Experts write and try to identify specific learned norms, values, and beliefs but there is much disagreement on whether the differences are deep-seated or superficial.
   Difficulty: hard
   Topic: Cultural Awareness

4. True   One example of a training program to enhance cross-cultural understanding is the Samsung Company that sends employees abroad for a year.
   Difficulty: hard
   Topic: Cultural Awareness

5. True   Consider the national anthem and your native flag and how this instills a feeling of national identity.
   Difficulty: easy
   Topic: The Nation as a Point of Reference

6. False   The same language increases communication, and this helps spread values and beliefs among a group.
   Difficulty: easy
   Topic: The Nation as a Point of Reference

7. False   Companies need to be aware how religious beliefs affect their product line.
   Difficulty: moderate
   Topic: Religion as a Cultural Stabilizer

8. False   Recent religious strife which affected businesses is violence among religious groups in the former Yugoslavia, Northern Ireland, and Lebanon, to mention a few.
   Difficulty: easy
   Topic: Religion as a Cultural Stabilizer

9. True   Max Weber considered the Protestant ethic an outgrowth of the Reformation which is when people viewed work as a means of salvation.
   Difficulty: hard
   Topic: Behavioral Practices Affecting Business

10. True   People tend to be more open to new products if they do not fear uncertainty.
    Difficulty: hard
    Topic: Risk-Taking Behavior

11. False   High-context cultures consider peripheral information valuable and therefore tend to engage in small talk more than low-context cultures.
Difficulty: hard
Topic: Obtaining Information

12. True   Ethnocentric individuals are culturally myopic.
Difficulty: moderate
Topic: Company and Management Orientations

13. False   It is false to say that relativism holds to a universal standard; the opposite is true.
Difficulty: hard
Topic: To Intervene or Not to Intervene

14. True   The Declaration of Human Rights lacks universal acceptance.
Difficulty: hard
Topic: To Intervene or Not to Intervene

15. True   The example shows the diverse interactions of cultures in a common meeting place for similar purposes.
Difficulty: moderate
Topic: The Globalization of Culture

Multiple Choice

1. a.   This case is a classic in showing the misunderstandings that can occur when a company is not aware of all the nuances of another culture when it is doing business in that environment.
Difficulty: easy
Topic: Introduction and PRI case

2. c.   The British did not understand the necessity of why Arabs considered this part of relationship building.
Difficulty: moderate
Topic: Cultural Awareness

3. c.   These are some of the more representative ways that culture is transmitted.
Difficulty: moderate
Topic: Cultural Formation and Dynamics

4. a.   All of the choices describe affiliations by birth.
Difficulty: hard
Topic: Behavioral Practices Affecting Business

5. c.   Although competence is a high value in the United States, other societies may consider affiliation with a certain ascribed group, seniority, or other factors of prime importance.
Difficulty: hard
Topic: Role of Competence

6. d.   Countries with high power distance include Guatemala, Panama, Malaysia, and the Philippines.
Difficulty: hard
Topic: Power Distance

7. b.   Collectivism is group-oriented, and a marketing strategy which focuses on group consensus would enhance success in this type of society.
Difficulty: moderate
Topic: Individualism versus Collectivism

8. a. An example is found in the Northern European culture that stresses finishing what one does before moving on to something else.
Difficulty: hard
Topic: Obtaining Information

9. d. Silent language is a complex set of cues used according to one's cultural norms.
Difficulty: hard
Topic: Silent Language

10. d. Culture shock can occur in a new cultural setting whether this is abroad or in one's home country. An example would be someone who moves from a small quiet village to a fast-paced city setting—wherever in the world they may be.
Difficulty: moderate
Topic: Culture Shock

11. c. An ethnocentric person ignores environmental differences in trying to implement home country systems into another setting.
Difficulty: moderate
Topic: Company and Management Orientations

12. a. These three methods are among the methods of effective strategies to institute change.
Difficulty: hard
Topic: Strategies for Instituting Change

13. c. The normative approach advocates intervention for international companies if ethical standards do not conform to the ideal or norm as perceived.
Difficulty: hard
Topic: Ethical Dilemmas and Social Responsibilities

14. a. This is an example of the legal conflicts and moral dilemmas international companies face when doing business in diverse places.
Difficulty: moderate
Topic: Ethical Dilemmas and Social Responsibilities

15. d. The examples given in the case show a commitment by Higgins to Japanese culture and management style. This indicates a polycentric orientation.
Difficulty: easy
Topic: Case: John Higgins

Chapter 3

The Political and Legal Environments Facing Business

CHAPTER OBJECTIVES

1. To discuss the different functions that political systems perform.

2. To compare democratic and totalitarian political regimes, and discuss how they can influence managerial decisions.

3. To describe how management can formulate and implement strategies to deal with foreign political environments.

4. To study the different types of legal systems and the legal relationships that exist between countries

5. To examine the major legal issues in international business.

TRUE/FALSE

1. A country's political system influences how business is conducted domestically but not how it is conducted internationally. T/F

   Hint   Consider how political and legal factors are part of the external environment that influences managerial decisions.

2. A political ideology rarely exists in developed countries. T/F

   Hint   Political ideologies are the body of complex ideas that constitute a sociopolitical program.

3. Most modern societies are pluralistic politically. T/F

   Hint   Pluralism allows different ideologies to coexist.

4. MNEs may be able to operate effectively in both democracies and totalitarian regimes. T/F

   Hint   MNEs operate in diverse political climates.

5. One of the signs of a democracy is that elected officials have limited terms. T/F

   Hint   Democracies value choice.

6. One of the major indicators of political rights is the existence of safeguards on the rights of majorities. T/F

   Hint   One criterion of political rights is the safeguarding of the rights of minorities.

7. One major indicator for civil liberties is the existence of a free press. T/F

   Hint   A free press allows for dissemination of political information.

8. All democratic governments require that all the people vote directly for their head of state. T/F

   Hint   Consider the differences in parliamentary systems around the world.

9. In theocratic totalitarianism, religious leaders are also the political leaders. T/F

   Hint   Consider that "theos" means "god."

10. Political risks tend to be more prevalent in totalitarian regimes. T/F

    Hint Totalitarian regimes are more likely to become unstable because of resistance movements.

11. Micro political risks are aimed at specific companies. T/F

    Hint Micro suggests that a smaller segment is targeted.

12. Communitarian paradigms are a communist form of government. T/F

    Hint Communitarian suggests an emphasis on group behavior and is not a political ideology.

13. Civil law is based on a detailed set of laws that make up a code. T/F

    Hint Civil law is also called a codified legal system.

14. Muslim countries use theocratic law as their legal system. T/F

    Hint Theocratic law systems are based on religious precepts.

15. Legal systems usually fall into three categories: common law, civil law, and theoretical law. T/F

    Hint Consider custom and precedent, legal codes, and religiously sanctioned law.

MULTIPLE CHOICE

1. Hong Kong was created under British rule in the 19th century as a consequence of:

   Hint Consider the mercantilist policies of the 19th century.

   a. a gift from the Chinese emperor.
   b. the Opium Wars which China lost to the British.
   c. a concession made by the Japanese.
   d. all of the above.

2. During the first 140 years of British rule in Hong Kong, an attempt to implement a representative democracy was:

   Hint Consider the political culture of the Hong Kong business elite.

   a. made during the Boxer rebellion.
   b. due to an American military tribunal.
   c. quashed by the local business elite which is sympathetic to totalitarian views.
   d. There was never an attempt to implement a democratic policy under British rule.

3. The ultimate test of any political system is its ability to:

   Hint Consider the pressures within a society.

   a. hold elections every two years.
   b. hold a society together despite pressures from different ideologies.
   c. both (a) and (b) are correct
   d. None of the answers are correct.

4. When considering the major indicators for civil liberties, one that is NOT a major indicator is:

   Hint   The indicators represent choices.

   a. equality under the law for select individuals.
   b. the existence of a free press.
   c. freedom from extreme governmental indifference or corruption.
   d. none of the above.

5. Emerging democracies are often fragile and unstable. Their instability stems from:

   Hint   Indonesia and the former republics of the Soviet Union are examples of this type of instability.

   a. internal division, corruption, power in the hands of a few, and destabilization from abroad.
   b. a two-party system.
   c. separation of church and state.
   d. a multi-party system.

6. A decentralized democratic system may make it difficult for companies because they may face conflicting laws. One example of this is:

   Hint   Consider the difference between state or provincial laws and federal laws.

   a. the political and legal system of France which is highly decentralized.
   b. the political and legal systems of Japan which is decentralized.
   c. both (a) and (b) are correct.
   d. the political and legal system of Canada, because it gives significant political power to the provinces, and, in many cases, the provinces have their own trade barriers.

7. Totalitarianism takes several forms, and they include:

   Hint   In a totalitarian state, a single party, individual, or group monopolizes political power.

   a. fascism, authoritarianism, and libertarianism.
   b. communism, fascism, and conservatism.
   c. the only form of totalitarianism is fascism.
   d. fascism, authoritarianism, communism, and theocratic totalitarianism are among the many forms of totalitarianism.

8. Political risks include:

   Hint   Political risks occur when the political climate in a foreign country changes in such a way that the company's operating position will deteriorate.

   a. internal political scandals.
   b. infrastructure building.
   c. civil disorder, change of leadership, and a change in alliances.
   d. none of the above.

9. A good example of how a communitarian philosophy can affect business is:

Hint   Communitarian countries establish a partnership with business.

   a.   best explained with the philosophy of survival of the fittest.
   b.   Japan's focus on supporting business by building infrastructure and establishing the MITI.
   c.   the United States' hands-off policy.
   d.   all of the above.

10. The legal system that is based on tradition, precedent, and custom is:

Hint   Tradition and custom indicate a common usage.

   a.   theocratic law.
   b.   civil law.
   c.   common law.
   d.   common code.

11. Laws on local business activities can influence both domestic and foreign companies in areas such as:

Hint   Legal and ethical issues often intertwine.

   a.   employment practices and contractual relationships only.
   b.   safety standards, consumerism, and environmental standards only.
   c.   in areas of health and safety standards, employment practices, antitrust prohibitions, and other critical social issues.
   d.   Legal issues are limited to domestic boundaries.

INTERNET EXERCISES

Exercise 1
International Chamber of Commerce (ICC)
http://www.iccwbo.org
Familiarize yourself with the following business topics: Business Law, Extortion and Bribery, Commercial Practices. In addition, read the announcements on the ICC main page, and reflect on the latest occurrences. Take a consulting role and write a briefing of your findings that addresses the most significant current political and legal issues in your findings.
Difficulty: moderate
Topic: Types and Causes of Political Risks

Exercise 2
China Today
http://www.chinatoday.com
Access the following topics: General Information, Government Agencies and Services, International Trade, and Law, Justice & Legal Services. Consider this information within the context of China's political system. Assess the political risk a company should consider in trading with China. Write a brief analysis of your findings.
Difficulty: moderate
Topic: Government Intervention in the Economy

Exercise 3
Swire Pacific Ltd.
http://eco-web.com
Click on "Countries" and access Swire's contacts in Hong Kong as well as other holdings in countries around the world. Relate this information to the opening case. Discuss how this relates to the changed political situation in Hong Kong as discussed in the opening case and Chapter 3.
Difficulty: hard
Topic: Case: The Taipan's Dilemma

Exercise 4
Bata web site
http://www.bata.com/
Read why Bata considers itself to be the "shoemaker of the world." Relate your findings to the end case in Chapter 3. Discuss what you have learned about Bata's strategy to survive in an international business environment.
Difficulty: easy
Topic: Case: Bata Shoe Organization

Exercise 5
China
http://www.chinatoday.com/
Taiwan
http://www.sinica.edu.tw/taiwan/
Compare these two nations who share a common history and tradition yet have opposing political ideologies. Discuss the similarities and the differences in their approach to business.
Difficulty: hard
Topic: Formulating and Implementing Political Strategies

CHAPTER 3 ANSWER KEY

True/False

1. **False**   Both domestic and international businesses continually monitor a country's political system and assess how it may affect the business climate.
   Difficulty: moderate
   Topic: The Political Environment

2. **False**   Political ideologies are prominent in developed countries, yet they tend to be suppressed to a large extent in totalitarian regimes.
   Difficulty: moderate
   Topic: Basic Political Ideologies

3. **True**   Modern societies that are not totalitarian politically support pluralism.
   Difficulty: easy
   Topic: Basic Political Ideologies

4. **True**   It is possible to operate effectively in all political systems, but the risks tend to be higher in less democratic countries.
   Difficulty: hard
   Topic: A Political Spectrum

5. **True**   Elections are an important part of the democratic process, and this allows for changing the elected officials on a regular basis.
   Difficulty: easy
   Topic: Democracy

6. **False**   Minorities have less power and therefore require protection and safeguards to ensure their political rights.
   Difficulty: moderate
   Topic: Political Rights and Civil Liberties

7. **True**   A free press is a key component of a free society.
   Difficulty: easy
   Topic: Political Rights and Civil Liberties

8. **False**   In the democratic United Kingdom, the ruling party selects the head of state.
   Difficulty: moderate
   Topic: Political Rights and Civil Liberties

9. **True**   Theocracies are by their very name led by religious leaders.
   Difficulty: easy
   Topic: Totalitarianism

10. **True**   Totalitarian regimes are threatened from resistance movements within and from political enemies outside and therefore tend to be less stable than democracies.
    Difficulty: easy
    Topic: Types and Causes of Political Risks

11. **True**   Companies may be targeted because of unethical or illegal practices that are counter to the regimes in power.
    Difficulty: moderate
    Topic: Micro and Macro Political Risks

12. False   Although communitarian suggests community, it is not necessarily communist.
     Difficulty: hard
     Topic: Government Intervention in the Economy

13. True   Civil laws are written down and used as codified guidelines.
     Difficulty: moderate
     Topic: Civil Law

14. True   Muslim countries use a prescribed legal system as is written in their sacred text, the Koran.
     Difficulty: moderate
     Topic: Theocratic Law

15. False   Common law, civil law, and theocratic law are the three legal systems.
     Difficulty: hard
     Topic: Kinds of Legal Systems

Multiple Choice

1.   b.   China's series of defeats in the Opium Wars resulted in the eventual loss of Chinese territory.
     Difficulty: moderate
     Topic: Case: The Taipan's Dilemma

2.   c.   The native business elite tends to favor a totalitarian view over democracy.
     Difficulty: hard
     Topic: Case: The Taipan's Dilemma

3.   b.   Different ideologies test a political system.
     Difficulty: moderate
     Topic: Basic Political Ideologies

4.   a.   This is not an indicator of civil liberties because it limits equality to only some instead of giving equality to all individuals.
     Difficulty: easy
     Topic: Political Rights and Civil Liberties

5.   a.   These are some of the major factors that have created instability to new democracies.
     Difficulty: hard
     Topic: Political Rights and Civil Liberties

6.   d.   Canadian laws give considerable weight to individual provinces.
     Difficulty: hard
     Topic: Political Rights and Civil Liberties

7.   d.   Totalitarianism may include a theocratic approach as well as an atheistic approach.
     Difficulty: hard
     Topic: Totalitarianism

8.   c.   These are serious signs of possible political risks.
     Difficulty: easy
     Topic: Types and Causes of Political Risk

9.   b.   Japan is a good example of using communitarian philosophy effectively.
     Difficulty: moderate
     Topic: Government Intervention in the Economy

10. c.   Courts use common law by basing decisions on precedent, custom, and usage.
      Difficulty: easy
      Topic: Kinds of Legal Systems

11. c.   This more extensive list shows some of the complexities of the international legal environment.
      Difficulty: hard
      Topic: Legal Issues in International Business

Chapter 4

The Economic Environment

CHAPTER OBJECTIVES

1. To learn the difference between the world's major economic systems.

2. To learn the criteria for dividing countries into different economic categories.

3. To discuss key economic issues that influence international business.

4. To assess the transition process certain countries are undertaking in changing to market economies—and how this transition affects international firms and managers.

TRUE/FALSE

1. One of the problems McDonald's faced in opening its restaurant in Moscow is that it was not in the Moscow City Council's five year-plan. T/F

   Hint   Command economies have set plans.

2. One of the benefits McDonald's experienced by locating a new restaurant in Moscow was the ease of securing local produce for its menu. T/F

   Hint   McDonald's has strict quality guidelines for produce.

3. Companies go abroad mainly to access factors of production or to benefit from demand conditions. T/F

   Hint   Consider production possibilities and sales potential.

4. Countries with low per-capita GNP and high populations are most desirable in terms of market potential. T/F

   Hint   Market potential is related to size of income and numbers of potential customers.

5. Gross domestic product (GDP) represents the value of all production that takes place within a nation's borders. T/F

   Hint   Consider the word domestic.

6. The World Bank is a multilateral lending agency. T/F

   Hint   The World Bank was established by the United Nations in 1944.

7. World Bank data tend to classify by GNP. T/F

   Hint   Geographic clusters such as South Asia and Latin America are frequently cited by the World Bank.

8. A market economy is one in which the state owns all the markets. T/F

   Hint   Market economy is synonymous with free market economy.

9. A command economy is also known as a centrally planned economy. T/F

   Hint   Command economies are run by the state.

10. Market socialism is a system found only in totalitarian countries. T/F

Hint   Market socialism is another example of a mixed economy.

11. The Asian Financial Crisis of 1997 was the result of the Japanese trade deficit. T/F

Hint   The 1997 Asian financial crises started in Thailand.

12. A drop in economic growth can have detrimental effects on investments. T/F

Hint   Slowing economic growth signals risk.

13. High rates of inflation tend to contribute to a country's falling currency rate. T/F

Hint   Inflation increases volume of money.

14. The balance of payments can be transactions between companies, government, or individuals. T/F

Hint   Balance of payments records a country's international transactions.

15. Privatization is an attempt by governments to buy privately owned enterprises. T/F

Hint   Privatization reduces government debt.

MULTIPLE CHOICE

1. The average number of customers served when McDonald's opened in Pushkin Square was:

Hint   The numbers increased a thousandfold from the count of the former restaurant in that location.

   a. McDonald's did not monitor the count.
   b. The customer count averaged 20,000 per day.
   c. The customer count averaged 5,000 per day.
   d. It was insignificant to the venture and therefore not reported.

2. Factors of production include the following essential conditions:

Hint   Consider the process and end product to determine the various factors needed.

   a. human resources or labor, physical resources such as land and weather, knowledge resources, capital and infrastructure such as roads, ports, and power.
   b. labor and capital only.
   c. human resources psychological resources and infrastructure.
   d. none of the above apply.

3. GNP and GDP differ in that:

Hint   Consider production outside of one's country and production within one's country.

   a. GNP represents the value of goods produced by domestic companies—at home or abroad, while GDP represents the value of goods produced by domestic companies at home.
   b. GNP and GDP mean the same thing.
   c. GNP measures all production within one nation, whereas GDP measures only the production of domestically owned firms.
   d. GNP measures the production of a nation's firms regardless of where this production takes place, and GDP represents the total production of all firms, foreign or domestic, within one country.

4. The World Bank uses per-capita GNP as a basis to:

   HintConsider the functions of the World Bank

   a. establish a basis for military aid.
   b. establish the foundation for investment disputes.
   c. lending policies.
   d. All of the above are correct.

5. High-income countries generate nearly 80% of the world's GNP, and they represent:

   Hint   The world has a disproportionate number of developing and emerging countries.

   a. a small number of countries and people.
   b. most of the countries in the Americas.
   c. Pacific Rim countries and the United States.
   d. both (a) and (b).

6. The Asian Financial Crisis of 1997 was precipitated by:

   Hint   Consider the domino effect of currency evaluation.

   a. economic growth in Vietnam.
   b. the earthquake in Japan.
   c. the devaluation of the Thai baht.
   d. all of the above.

7. The lack of financial transparency has been cited as a major problem that contributed to the Asian Financial Crisis. This asserts that:

   Hint   Consider the need for thorough financial analysis.

   a. the banking systems did not have up-to-date technology.
   b. financial statements were overly thorough which caused confusion in interpreting them.
   c. both (a) and (b) are correct.
   d. instead of analyzing financial data, many lenders tended to make decisions based on influence peddling and corruption.

8. Management needs to consider the consequences of inflation because:

   Hint   Consider that inflation connotes expansion.

   a. prices will fall significantly.
   b. exchange rates stabilize, resulting in a reduction of risk.
   c. inflation often results in a decrease in interest rates.
   d. none of the above is correct.

9. The balance of payments records a country's international transactions between:

   Hint   Consider the word balance and payments and who would be affected.

   a. companies and individuals.
   b. the merchandise trade balance, which measures the country's trade deficit or surplus.
   c. companies, government, or individuals.
   d. all of the above.

10. Some of the most heavily indebted countries in the world in terms of total debt are:

Hint   Developing countries tend to have large debts.

a.   Brazil, Mexico, and Indonesia.
b.   Japan, Brazil, and Indonesia.
c.   Saudi Arabia, Japan, and Russia.
d.   none of the above.

11. The internal debt of a country is the result of:

Hint   Consider government spending beyond revenues.

a.   a number of reasons which include: poorly run tax systems, excessive losses on state-owned enterprises, military expenditures, and social programs.
b.   an effective privatization program.
c.   both (a) and (b).
d.   none of the above.

12. The term "chaebol" describes:

Hint   It describes a Korean business entity.

a.   the chairman of a Korean company.
b.   a Korean large business conglomerate such as the Daewoo Group.
c.   a symbolic rite within the Korean culture.
d.   all of the above.

13. The impact of the fall of the Thai baht on Korea was partly a result of:

Hint   Korea had a large foreign debt.

a.   the Korean won being pegged on the baht.
b.   Korea's dependence on Thai tourism.
c.   Korea was not affected by the Thai crisis.
d.   none of the above.

INTERNET EXERCISES

Exercise 1
McDonald's web site
http://www.mcdonalds.com
Select Russia from the country sites. What are the estimated sales figures to date? How many restaurants does McDonald's operate in Russia to date? How many people are employed there? Consider the costs and benefits of this venture. Discuss.
Difficulty: easy
Topic: Case: McDonald's Corporation

Exercise 2
McDonald's web site
http://www.mcdonalds.com
Visit a minimum of two other country locations. Consider the differences with each country's political and economic system. Compare the success of each. What do you attribute to be the success factors for each country location? What are the risks? Take the role of a consultant, and advise McDonald's on potential economic risks associated with these locations.
Difficulty: hard
Topic: An Economic Description of Countries

Exercise 3
World Bank
http://www.worldbank.org
Get to know the bank at work, resources, and partners. Write an essay and give a succinct overview of the World Bank and its activities.
Difficulty: moderate
Topic: Countries Classified by Income

Exercise 4
World Bank
http://www.worldbank.org
Explore the IBDR, IDA, IFC, MIGA, and ICSID. Briefly describe the main functions of each organization.
Difficulty: easy
Topic: Countries Classified by Economic System

Exercise 5
Daewoo
http://www.Daewoo.com
Study their company profile. Consider their activities around the globe and their economic viability overall. Discuss your view of Daewoo's contribution to the economic stability to Korea, and Asia in general. Is Daewoo a key player? Why or why not?
Difficulty: hard
Topic: Case: The Daewoo Group and the Asian Financial Crisis

CHAPTER 4 ANSWER KEY

True/False

1. True   Early negotiation attempts by McDonald's with the Moscow City Council were frustrated because the McDonald's proposals were not in the pre-set five-year plan.
   Difficulty: moderate
   Topic: Case: McDonald's Corporation

2. False   McDonald's had to implement a program to educate local farmers to grow and raise many products that were not available.
   Difficulty: moderate
   Topic: Case: McDonald's Corporation

3. True   These considerations drive decisions to go international.
   Difficulty: moderate
   Topic: An Economic Description of Countries

4. False   Good market potential is a medium or high per-capita GNP and a medium to high population base.
   Difficulty: moderate
   Topic: Countries Classified by Income

5. True   GDP includes the value of all production within a given country regardless if it is done by a domestic or foreign firm.
   Difficulty: easy
   Topic: Countries Classified by Income

6. True   The World Bank is comprised of 181 countries.
   Difficulty: moderate
   Topic: Countries Classified by Income

7. False   The World Bank has established regional classifications such as East and Central Europe, Central Asia, Sub-Saharan Africa, etc.
   Difficulty: moderate
   Topic: Countries Classified by Region

8. False   It is false to assert that the state controls a market economy.
   Difficulty: easy
   Topic: Market Economy

9. True   Command economies are centrally planned and are represented by countries such as China and Cuba.
   Difficulty: moderate
   Topic: Command Economy

10. False   It is false to assume that market socialism is dominant in totalitarian regimes.
    Difficulty: hard
    Topic: Mixed Economy

11. False   The Asian financial crisis did not start in Japan; it was the result of the devaluation of the Thai baht in July of 1997.
    Difficulty: hard
    Topic: Asian Financial Crisis

12. True   An example of curtailed investments because of a drop in economic growth is illustrated by McDonald's in Moscow.
Difficulty: moderate
Topic: Economic Growth

13. True   Inflation is a significant factor that influences exchange rates.
Difficulty: hard
Topic: Inflation

14. True   Balance of payments tends to represent diverse international transactions.
Difficulty: moderate
Topic: Surpluses and Deficits

15. False   Privatization frees enterprises from government ownership.
Difficulty: easy
Topic: Internal Debt and Privatization

Multiple Choice

1. b.   The customer count from the former restaurant was 200 per day, and McDonald's increased that to 20,000 per day.
Difficulty: moderate
Topic: Case: McDonald's Corporation

2. a.   These are the classic factors of production.
Difficulty: moderate
Topic: An Economic Description of Countries

3. d.   GNP measures a country's income by looking at production inside and outside of its borders, while GDP measures all domestic production.
Difficulty: hard
Topic: Countries Classified by Income

4. c.   GNP data are important tools to establish lending guidelines.
Difficulty: moderate
Topic: Countries Classified by Income

5. a.   There are a relatively small number of high-income countries in the world.
Difficulty: easy
Topic: Countries Classified by Income

6. c.   When the government of Thailand freed the baht from currency control, the baht fell 17% against the U.S. dollar and triggered a currency crisis in Asia and impacted investments.
Difficulty: hard
Topic: Asian Financial Crisis

7. d.   It was often said that the best way to make a loan was to take the borrower to lunch and a round of golf instead of analyzing the financial data. This resulted in loose controls.
Difficulty: hard
Topic: Asian Financial Crisis

8. d.   None of the responses are correct.
Difficulty: hard
Topic: Inflation

9. **c.** This rather broad definition generalizes the balance of payment concept.
   Difficulty: moderate
   Topic: Surpluses and Deficits

10. **a.** Total debt for Brazil was measured by the IMF to be \$179.0 billion, Mexico's debt was \$157.1 billion, and Indonesia's debt was \$129.0 billion.
    Difficulty: easy
    Topic: External Debt

11. **a.** The reasons stated are among the major reasons for internal debts.
    Difficulty: easy
    Topic: Internal Debt and Privatization

12. **b.** A chaebol is a common Korean form for a family-owned business conglomerate.
    Difficulty: easy
    Topic: Case: The Daewoo Group and the Asian Financial Crisis

13. **d.** The other responses do not accurately portray the impact of the crisis. A major reason for Korea's difficulties as a result of the falling baht was that it initiated a reaction in the world money markets with the result of increasing interest rate. Korea that was dependent on low-interest foreign loans faced an inflated debt load as a result.
    Difficulty: hard
    Topic: Case: The Daewoo Group and the Asian Financial Crisis

Chapter 5

International Trade Theory

CHAPTER OBJECTIVES

1. To explain trade theories.

2. To discuss how global efficiencies can be increased through free trade.

3. To introduce prescriptions for altering trade patterns.

4. To explore how business decisions influence international trade.

TRUE/FALSE

1. Sri Lanka has only recently emerged into the area of international trade. T/F

   Hint   Consider Sri Lanka's strategic location to other markets.

2. Until 1975, over half of Sri Lanka's export earnings were from rubber. T/F

   Hint   Sri Lanka's name under British rule was Ceylon, and this name was popularized in referring to a staple British drink.

3. Import substitution was one of the trade policies Sri Lanka implemented in the 1960s. T/F

   Hint   Import substitution concentrates on local production.

4. Trade policies impact business decisions. T/F

   Hint   Trade policies are established by governments and determine what, how much, and with whom their country should trade.

5. Descriptive trade theories are not considered valid decision-making tools. T/F

   Hint   Descriptive trade theories ask how much, which products, and with whom a country will trade in the absence of restrictions.

6. According to mercantilist theory, countries should import more than they export. T/F

   Hint   Mercantilism sought to enrich and empower the governments of newly emerging nation states.

7. The term *neomercantilism* can describe countries that try to run favorable balances of trade. T/F

   Hint   Neo means new.

8. Acquired advantage goes hand in hand with natural advantage within the concept of the absolute advantage trade theory. T/F

   Hint   Natural is innate and acquired requires a process.

34

9. It is possible for a country to have a comparative advantage and have a natural disadvantage at the same time. T/F

   Hint   Comparative advantage considers production efficiency whereas a natural advantage considers innate resources.

10. Countries with large economies and high per capita incomes are most likely to produce goods that use technologies requiring long production runs. T/F

   Hint   Local markets are key considerations when considering costly production runs.

11. The factor-proportion theory expands on the theories of Adam Smith and David Ricardo. T/F

   Hint   Consider natural advantages and efficiency in production.

12. The Product Life Cycle Theory of Trade focuses on global lifestyle issues. T/F

   Hint   Consider the life cycle of a product from beginning to end.

13. In the decline stage of the Product Life Cycle trade theory the production is moved to the emerging new markets. T/F

   Hint   Consider transportation costs.

14. When a company reduces its costs by 20 to 30% each time it doubles its output, this phenomenon is called: use of excess capacity. T/F

   Hint   An increase in output over time is based on efficiency due to experience.

15. The cashew industry in India benefited from the fact that manual dexterity was an important factor in the processing of cashews. T/F

   Hint   Indian children make handicrafts at home.

MULTIPLE CHOICE

1. Sri Lanka developed three specific trade policies since 1960. They include ALL BUT the following:

   Hint   It was a progressive trade policy to diversify products and markets.

   a.   1960–1977, import substitution.
   b.   1977–1988, strategic trade policy.
   c.   1988–1995, intensified former colonial ties with British markets to narrow trade relations.
   d.   1988–present, strategic trade policy, along with openness to imports.

2. Sri Lanka is typical of most emerging economies but atypical in that the country has:

   Hint   Sri Lanka has a high quality of life.

   a.   a high death rate.
   b.   a high illiteracy rate.
   c.   poor health care standards.
   d.   a high quality of life, which includes a high literacy rate, good nutrition and health standards, equality of income distribution, and low population growth.

3. Sri Lanka exports include:

   Hint   Exports include services and products.

   a.   Sri Lankan labor from its workers working abroad and foreign tourists visiting Sri Lanka.
   b.   Sri Lanka tourists visiting foreign countries.
   c.   foreigners earning an income within Sri Lanka.
   d.   None of the above is correct.

4. Prescriptive theories about international trade prescribe whether governments should:

   Hint   Consider policies that direct trade.

   a.   interfere with the free movement of goods and services among countries to alter the amount, composition, and direction of trade.
   b.   examine and explain trade patterns under laissez-faire conditions.
   c.   prescribe domestic production.
   d.   Both (a) and (c) are correct.

5. Mercantilism advocated that:

   Hint   Mercantilism empowered central governments to invest in armies and national institutions.

   a.   merchants not governments conduct commerce.
   b.   countries should export more than they import.
   c.   colonies become self-sufficient.
   d.   colonies establish manufacturing facilities.

6. The theory of absolute advantage was developed by:

   Hint   The theory of absolute advantage was profiled in the book titled *Wealth of Nations*.

   a.   Karl Marx.
   b.   David Ricardo.
   c.   Adam Smith.
   d.   Eli Hecksher and Bertil Ohlin.

7. The theory of comparative advantage as advocated by David Ricardo maintains that:

   Hint   Selection and concentration on the most efficient process is key to comparative advantage.

   a.   factor endowments create comparative advantage.
   b.   self-sufficiency gives countries an advantage.
   c.   a country gains from trade if it specializes in those products that it can produce more efficiently than other products.
   d.   David Ricardo did not develop the comparative advantage theory.

8. Some of the limitations of the theories of specialization include:

   Hint   Consider country specific variables.

   a.   cultural differences.
   b.   civil strife.
   c.   transportation costs.
   d.   All of the above are correct.

9. The factor-proportions theory developed by Heckscher and Ohlin states that:

   Hint   Factors of production include: land, labor and capital.

   a. differences in countries' endowments of labor compared to their endowments of land or capital explained differences in the cost of production factors.
   b. a proportion of a county's factories needed to concentrate on innovation.
   c. Both (a) and (b) are correct.
   d. None of the above is correct.

10. The country-similarities theory states that:

    Hint   Consider similar needs and markets

    a. companies test foreign markets before developing a product in order to create products similar to their needs.
    b. countries similar in size have similar needs.
    c. similarity in political ideologies is necessary for trade.
    d. None of the above is true.

11. The most recent instances of economic near-independence have been noted in:

    Hint   Consider traditional self-sufficient societies.

    a. Japan prior to WWII.
    b. the Liawep tripe found in Papua New Guinea in 1993, and in present-day Bhutan.
    c. Saudi Arabia once it became oil rich.
    d. Both (a) and (c) are correct.

12. The two basic approaches to government policy are to:

    Hint   Governments look for improvements in the domestic arena to protect industry.

    a. instigate embargoes and trade wars.
    b. ask for UN sanctions and increase tariffs.
    c. alter conditions that will affect industry in general and alter conditions that will affect targeted industry.
    d. establish bilateral agreements and threaten trade sanctions.

13. Singapore has been losing its competitive advantage because of:

    Hint   Consider the high cost of living in Singapore.

    a. its rising labor costs.
    b. high crime rate.
    c. civil disorder.
    d. high illiteracy rate.

14. India's cashew-processing industry developed in response to:

    Hint   The Indian diet consists of many vegetarian dishes.

    a. religious symbolism in India.
    b. the Indian consumer's demand for cashews.
    c. the cashew's conversion to industrial oil for India's industry.
    d. None of the above is correct.

INTERNET EXERCISES

Exercise 1.
Sri Lankan Trade
http://www.ccom.lk/
Reflect on the Sri Lanka Case and consider that country's development and trade strategies over the last 40 years. Explore the diverse links within this site. Visit the Sri Lanka Business section and gain an understanding of the opportunities and business climate. Write an essay that gives an overview of Sri Lanka and assess the trading opportunities this country offers to business outside of its borders.

Exercise 2.
Mercantilism
http://www.pei-intl.com/THEORY/MERCHANT.HTM
Read the brief overview of mercantilism. Search for other sites that discuss this topic. Search for additional sites that discuss neomercantilism. Compare and contrast the old and new version of mercantilism in a brief essay. Summarize your essay by discussing how these concepts affect government policymakers and business decision makers with regard to international trade.

Exercise 3.
Farm World
http://www.farmworld.com/a/fw4010.html
In order to understand the complexity of agricultural commodities on the world market, explore the Farm World Web site fully. What can you learn from this site as it relates to policies and procedures? What information can you find on the cashew nut, and how does it relate to the trade theories discussed in this chapter and the Cashew nut case? Write a synopsis of your findings.

Exercise 4.
India
http://www.webindia.com/
Explore the Business Stories and Trade sections. Using the Porter Diamond model, discuss which areas give India a competitive advantage. Include products as well as services. Support your views with information obtained from the Web site.

Exercise 5.
Western India Cashew Company
http://www.cashewkernels.com/
Relate your findings from the Web site to the Cashew Case and discuss how the information compares with the case and the trade theories you have studied in this chapter. Which trade theory would you use to explain the Cashew Case? Be specific.

CHAPTER 5 ANSWER KEY

True/False

1. **False**   Sri Lanka has traded its agricultural products, some minerals, and livestock as an independent nation and for a period of time as a British colony.
   Difficulty: moderate
   Topic: Case: Sri Lankan Trade

2. **False**   Rubber was not the focal point of agriculture in Sri Lanka, instead, the main cash crop during British rule and up to the 1970s was tea.
   Difficulty: moderate
   Topic: Case: Sri Lankan Trade

3. **True**   Yes, in order to build local industry, Sri Lanka encouraged local production of goods and services that would otherwise be imported.
   Difficulty: hard
   Topic: Case: Sri Lankan Trade

4. **True**   Yes, business decisions assess the impact a country's trade policies will have on them.
   Difficulty: moderate
   Topic: Introduction

5. **False**   Descriptive trade theories are indeed useful and necessary in assessing opportunities and risks in international trade.
   Difficulty: hard
   Topic: Introduction

6. **False**   According to mercantilism trade theory, countries should export more than they import and receive gold from countries rather than reciprocal trade.
   Difficulty: hard
   Topic: Mercantilism

7. **True**   Yes, countries that encourage a favorable balance of trade by curtailing imports are sometimes labeled as being neomercantilist.
   Difficulty: hard
   Topic: Mercantilism

8. **False**   Yes, acquired advantage is related to production processes, whereas natural advantage is related to natural found factors of production such as fertile land and a healthy labor force.
   Difficulty: moderate
   Topic: Absolute Advantage

9. **True**   Yes, a country may have developed an efficient processing method for a particular good even though the materials for this good are not naturally found in its country.
   Difficulty: hard
   Topic: Comparative Advantage

10. **True**   Yes, a country's size and income determines markets and this reduces risks when undertaking expensive production runs.
    Difficulty: moderate
    Topic: Theory of Country Size

11. True   Yes, this theory considers land, labor, capital, and the most efficient use of these resources in establishing a country's comparative advantage.
    Difficulty: hard
    Topic: Factor-Proportion Theory

12 False   Yes it is false to simplify the Product Life Cycle Theory of Trade into lifestyle issues only.
    Difficulty: easy
    Topic: The Product Life Cycle Theory of Trade

13. True   Yes, the theory states that a declining demand in the original country of production and increasing demand in new markets abroad tends to encourage movement of production to the countries where demand is increasing.
    Difficulty: moderate
    Topic: The Product Life Cycle of Trade

14. False   Yes, it is incorrect to assume that reducing costs is a use of excess capacity.
    Difficulty: hard
    Topic: Strategic Advantages of Exports

15. True   Manual dexterity is learned at an early age in India
    Difficulty: moderate
    Topic: Case: The Cashew

Multiple Choice

1. c.   No, Sri Lanka political leaders sought to reduce dependence on British markets rather than increase them.
    Difficulty: hard
    Topic: Case: Sri Lankan Trade

2. d.   Yes, Sri Lanka has an exemplary quality of life among emerging economies.
    Difficulty: moderate
    Topic: Case: Sri Lankan Trade

3. a.   Yes the earnings from Sri Lankan workers abroad and tourists visiting the country represent service exports.
    Difficulty: hard
    Topic: Case: Sri Lankan Trade

4. a.   Yes, this definition reflects a prescriptive trade theory.
    Difficulty: hard
    Topic: Introduction

5. b.   Yes, mercantilism imposed restrictions on most imports and subsidized production of many products that could otherwise not compete in domestic or export markets.
    Difficulty: moderate
    Topic: Mercantilism

6. c.   Yes, Adam Smith developed the theory of absolute advantage in his book titled *Wealth of Nations*.
    Difficulty: easy
    Topic: Absolute Advantage

7. c.   Yes, comparative advantage advocates specialization based on productivity.
    Difficulty: hard
    Topic: Comparative Advantage

8.   c.   Yes, transportation costs can negate the advantages of specialization by increasing the price of a good by the transportation and handling costs.
Difficulty: easy
Topic: Some Assumptions and Limitations of the Theories of Specialization

9.   a.   Yes, this summarizes the factor-proportions theory.
Difficulty: easy
Topic: Factor-Proportions Theory

10.   d.   Yes all of the above are false. The country-similarity theory says that once a company has developed a new product in response to observed market conditions in the home market, it will turn to markets it sees as most similar to those at home.
Difficulty: hard
Topic: Country Similarity Theory

11.   b.   Yes the isolation from other societies required strategies making them self-sufficient.
Difficulty: easy
Topic: Degree of Dependence

12.   c. Yes, these general approaches are basic to government policy regarding trade.
Difficulty: moderate
Topic: Strategic Trade Policy

13.   a.   Yes, Singapore's high labor cost has diminished its competitive advantage in manufacturing.
Difficulty: easy
Topic: Strategic Trade Policy

14.   b.   Yes, a strong domestic market for cashews stimulated the domestic cashew-processing industry in India.
Difficulty: easy
Topic: Case: The Cashew

Chapter 6

Governmental Influence on Trade

CHAPTER OBJECTIVES

1. To evaluate the rationale for governmental policies that enhance and restrict trade.

2. To examine the effects of pressure groups on trade policies.

3. To compare the protectionist arguments used in developed countries with those used in developing ones.

4. To study the potential and actual effects of governmental intervention on the free flow of trade.

5. To give an overview of the major means by which trade is restricted, regulated, and liberalized.

6. To examine the World Trade Organization.

7. To show that governmental trade policies create business uncertainties.

TRUE/FALSE

1. The Banana War focused on the EU's attempt to protect the Caribbean-based banana because these bananas are superior in food value. T/F

    Hint   Growers and distributors lobby government for favorable trade policies.

2. Protectionism is a term that represents government measures that attempt to protect domestic industries from foreign competition. T/F

    Hint   Protection means security.

3. Government protectionist policies often conflict in satisfying the intended economic, social, and political objectives they were created for. T/F

    Hint   Consider the consequences of the banana war.

4. Governmental intervention in trade is purely motivated by economics. T/F

    Hint   Trade has economic and social consequences.

5. Restricting imports in order to create domestic jobs creates risks in international trade. T/F

    Hint   Retaliation is likely when trade restrictions are imposed.

6. The Infant-Industry Arguments holds that a government should subsidize new industries. T/F

    Hint   Infants are vulnerable and need protection.

7. The automobile industries in Brazil and South Korea are examples of government protection for infant industries. T/F

    Hint   Brazil and Korea have successful automobile industries.

8. Import substitution refers to a government's policy to substitute imports for locally produced goods. T/F

    Hint   Import substitution is a protectionist policy.

9. The U.S. government restricted France Telecom and Deutsche Telekom in the U.S. telephone market because AT&T had a monopoly in the United States. T/F

    Hint   Consider comparable access or "fairness."

10. *Dumping* as a term in international trade refers to illegally dumping toxic waste products. T/F

    Hint   *Dumping* as a trade term refers to price.

11. The essential-industry argument in trade refers to a government's concern to protect industries that are essential to that country's survival as a nation. T/F

    Hint   Consider products for military use.

12. Tariffs may be collected by the exporting country or the importing country. T/F

    Hint   Consider transit tariffs and duty.

13. Subsidies are nontariff barriers. T/F

    Hint   Subsidies give an advantage to the producer.

14. Standards are a form of nontariff barrier. T/F

    Hint   Set standards limit access to certain markets.

15. The Helms-Burton bill was created to enhance relations with non-U.S. companies that trade with Cuba. T/F

    Hint   The Helms-Burton bill addresses past grievances with the Castro government.

MULTIPLE CHOICE

1. When studying governmental influence on trade, the banana war in the beginning chapter case represents:

    Hint   Consider the complexity of multiple stakeholders in international trade.

    a.   government influence and complex lobbying among major stakeholders.
    b.   the competitive edge of the banana as a product.
    c.   the Porter Diamond theory of trade.
    d.   the absolute advantage of banana growers in the Caribbean

2. The EU banana policy resulted in:

    Hint   Consider pricing and protectionism

    a.   helping former colonies sell bananas and reducing the price of imported bananas.
    b.   helping the banana growers worldwide.
    c.   help to poor former colonies and increase in banana prices in the EU.
    d.   None of the above is correct.

3.   Economic rationales for governmental intervention includes:

Hint   Governmental interventions are classified as economic or noneconomic.

    a.   the argument to maintain essential industries.
    b.   unemployment and preserving culture issues.
    c.   unemployment and the infant-industry argument.
    d.   Both (a) and (c) are correct.

4.   When the United States countered France's prohibition of U.S. hormone-treated beef by placing additional taxes on French cheese and foie gras, it was retaliating under the principle of:

Hint   Consider fairness and reciprocity.

    a.   comparable access or fairness.
    b.   price-control objectives.
    c.   dumping.
    d.   None of the above is correct.

5.   The optimum-tariff theory holds that:

Hint   Optimizing may require adjustments.

    a.   foreign producers will increase prices to counter the imposed tariffs.
    b.   a foreign producer will lower prices to counter the import tariff.
    c.   there is no such theory.
    d.   an importing country adds a specific duty on each unit.

6.   Noneconomic rationales for government interventions include all BUT the following:

Hint   Noneconomic reasons for trade barriers are concerned about national survival and identity.

    a.   maintenance of defense industries.
    b.   prevention of shipments to unfriendly countries.
    c.   conservation of activities that help preserve a national identity.
    d.   None of the above is correct.

7.   Compound duty is a combination of:

Hint   Consider the two main types of tariffs.

    a.   transit tariff and specific duty.
    b.   subsidies and ad valorem duty.
    c.   specific duty and ad valorem duty.
    d.   There is no such term as *compound duty*.

8.   Subsidies are a form of:

Hint   Subsidies are directed to domestic producers.

    a.   tariff.
    b.   foreign aid.
    c.   nontariff barrier.
    d.   reciprocal agreement among governments.

9. "Buy local" legislation is considered:

    Hint Buying locally produced goods reduces demand for foreign goods.

    a. a tariff barrier.
    b. a form of quantitative control and a nontariff barrier.
    c. illegal by the WTO.
    d. Both (a) and (b) are correct.

10. A set of classifications used as a nontariff barrier are generally recognized as:

    Hint Consider issues such as pollution-control devices in automobiles.

    a. standards that are generally recognized as viable nontariff barriers.
    b. administrative delays.
    c. Both (a) and (b) are correct.
    d. None of the above is correct.

11. The lengthy delays, sometimes taking 30 days or more to clear imported merchandise in South Korea, is a type of nontariff barrier referred to as:

    Hint The delays are often approved by local government administrators.

    a. embargoes.
    b. administrative delays.
    c. quotas.
    d. reciprocal requirements.

12. The General Agreement of Tariffs and Trade (GATT), formed by 23 countries in 1947, was the forerunner of:

    Hint GATT was created to address trade restrictions and to help ease world trade.

    a. the United Nations (UN).
    b. the World Trade Organization (WTO).
    c. NAFTA.
    d. GATT still functions and has not been replaced.

13. Ethical dilemmas concerning embargoes can be illustrated with the example in:

    Hint Trade policies affect many different layers within a society.

    a. Germany after WWII and the Marshal Plan.
    b. There are no known trade embargoes. It is a medieval term.
    c. the sanctions against Iraq.
    d. None of the above is correct.

INTERNET EXERCISES

Exercise 1.
Banana Action
http://bananas.agoranet.be/
Visit the Banana Action Web site and identify the stakeholders. What is the intent of the site? Who benefits from this site? Who is criticized on this site? How does this site relate to protectionism? Write a succinct overview and relate it to the Banana War case.

Exercise 2.

Embargo

Search the Web with the word "embargo." Note the many different sites that discuss embargoes around the world. Visit at least four different sites and give a brief overview of each site. Summarize by discussing the relationship between embargoes and protectionism. Who benefits from embargoes? Who loses?

Exercise 3.

World Trade Organization

http://www.wto.org

Visit the World Trade Organization site and peruse the Trade Policy Reviews and Dispute Settlements under Trade Topics. What are the issues here? How do these topics relate to protectionism? Summarize by discussing who you consider to be the winners and the losers in these disputes.

Exercise 4.

World Trade Organization

http://www.wto.org/

Visit the World Trade Organization Web site and familiarize yourself with the topics under Resources. Write a succinct overview of your findings in this section with the objective of explaining some of the functions of the WTO.

Exercise 5.

Cuba

http://www.cubaweb.com/

Visit the Cuba Web page and familiarize yourself with Cuba. Visit the Business Library on this site and read the "Cuban News" section and the "U.S. Laws dealing with Cuba" section. Go to the "U.S. Embargo" section and other areas of interest. Write a succinct overview of your finding. How does this relate to the United States-Cuban Trade case? How does this relate to embargoes? Connect these issues to government influence on trade.

CHAPTER 6 ANSWER KEY

True/False

1. False   Yes, it is false to assume that the banana war was a nutritional issue.   Rather, it represents governments seeking to protect strong banana lobbies.
    Difficulty: moderate
    Topic: The Banana War

2. True   Yes, protectionist policies seek to guard against foreign competition.
    Difficulty: easy
    Topic: Introduction

3. True   Yes, protectionist policies tend to have conflicting results in real practice.
    Difficulty: moderate
    Topic: Conflicting Results of Trade Policies

4. False   Governments intervene in trade for economic and noneconomic reasons.
    Difficulty: moderate
    Topic: Economic Rationales for Governmental Intervention

5. True   Yes, retaliation is likely when a country puts up trade barriers.
    Difficulty: moderate
    Topic: Economic Rationales for Governmental Intervention

6. False   No, the Infant-Industry Argument holds that a government should guarantee an emerging industry a large share of the domestic market until the industry becomes efficient enough to compete against imports.
    Difficulty: moderate
    Topic: Infant-Industry Argument

7. True   Yes, the Brazilian and Korean governments protected their automobile industries from competitors during their industry's infancy.
    Difficulty: easy
    Topic: Infant-Industry Argument

8. False   Yes, it is not correct to say that import substitution targets imports instead of domestically produced goods. The reverse is the case.
    Difficulty: moderate
    Topic: Import Substitution versus Export Promotion

9. False   Yes, this was not a monopoly issue, but rather a fairness in access issue with France and Germany.
    Difficulty: hard
    Topic: Comparable Access or "Fairness"

10. False   Yes, although disposing of toxic waste is a global problem, the term *dumping* in trade refers to unfair pricing.
    Difficulty: hard
    Topic: Economic Relationships with Other Countries

11. True   Yes, a government may protect essential industries such as certain food crops or military related products to assure a domestic supply.
    Difficulty: moderate
    Topic: Noneconomic Rationale for Government Intervention

12. True   Yes, tariffs may be charged when goods pass through a country as well as when they enter a country.
    Difficulty: hard
    Topic: Tariffs

13. True   Yes, a country may subsidize a producer giving the producer an advantage over foreign competitors.
    Difficulty: hard
    Topic: Subsidies

14. True   Yes, the use of standards is an effective barrier to trade.
    Difficulty: hard
    Topic: Standards

15. False   Yes, this bill signed in 1996 addresses past grievances with the Castro government, which seized property owned by U.S. citizens in Cuba and furthermore looks unfavorably on companies who use this confiscated property today.
    Difficulty: hard
    Topic: The Helms-Burton Law

Multiple Choice

1. a.   Yes, the banana case shows how governments are caught between numerous stakeholders when influencing decisions on trade.
   Difficulty: easy
   Topic: The Banana War

2. c.   Yes, the protectionist policies reduced competition for bananas in the EU and resulted in higher prices for the EU consumers.
   Difficulty: moderate
   Topic: Conflicting Results of Trade Policies

3. c.   Yes, these are some of the primary economic concerns of governments when considering trade interventions.
   Difficulty: moderate
   Topic: Economic Rationales for Governmental Intervention

4. a.   Yes, governments are sensitive to fairness in trade and tend to retaliate if fairness becomes an issue.
   Difficulty: moderate
   Topic: Comparable Access or "Fairness"

5. b.   Yes, this describes the theory correctly.
   Difficulty: hard
   Topic: Economic Relationships with Other Countries

6. d.   Yes, all the examples given above are noneconomic rationales used by governments to enforce trade barriers.
   Difficulty: moderate
   Topic: Noneconomic Rationales for Government Intervention

7. c.   Yes, specific duty that assesses a tariff on a per unit basis and ad valorem duty that assess a tariff as a percentage, when combined represent the term *compound duty*.
   Difficulty: moderate
   Topic: Tariffs

8.   c.   Yes, subsidies are used to create pricing advantages for domestic producers that, in turn, create barriers on foreign producers.
      Difficulty: easy
      Topic: Nontariff Barriers: Direct Price Influences

9.   b.   Yes, "buy local" legislation is an effective form of non-tariff barrier when used by government procurement offices because it reduces foreign purchases by governments.
      Difficulty: easy
      Topic: Nontariff Barriers: Quantity Controls

10.   a.   Yes, standards such as labeling and testing standards allow the sales of domestic products, but may inhibit foreign-made ones.
      Difficulty: easy
      Topic: Nontariff Barriers: Quantity Controls

11.   b.   Yes, the practice by local officials that delays processing of imported goods is called administrative delays.
      Difficulty: moderate
      Topic: Nontariff Barriers: Quantity Controls

12.   b.   Yes, the WTO, officially formed in 1995 has taken the place of GATT.
      Difficulty: moderate
      Topic: Functions of the WTO

13.   c.   Yes, the sanctions aimed at the Iraq regime, unfortunately they also impact innocent civilians.
      Difficulty: moderate
      Topic: Ethical Dilemmas and Social Responsibilities

Chapter 7

Regional Economic Integration and Cooperative Agreements

CHAPTER OBJECTIVES

1.   To define different forms of economic integration and how it affects international business.

2.   To describe the static and dynamic effects and the trade creation and diversion dimensions of economic integration.

3.   To present different trading groups, such as the European Union (EU), the North American Free Trade Agreement (NAFTA), and Asia-Pacific Economic Cooperation (APEC).

4.   To describe the rationale for success of commodity agreements.

5.   To discuss the effects of economic integration on the environment.

TRUE/FALSE

1.   Ford Motor Company's marketing strategy in Europe reflects a company that saw Europe as distinctly fragmented into narrow markets within their specific nation states. T/F

     Hint   Ford was among the first to recognize that Europe was one common market.

2.   The United States can be considered as a good example for regional economic integration. T/F

     Hint   Regional Economic Integration tends to include a common currency labor and factor mobility at an advanced stage.

3.   Regional economic integration is the political and economic agreements among countries that give preference to member countries to that agreement. T/F

     Hint   Integration tends for cohesion.

4.   Regional trading groups are of little concern to MNEs. T/F

     Hint   Regional trading groups define market size and set trade policy.

5.   The WTO allows a departure from its policy to grant the same favorable trade conditions to all WTO members in the case of regional trade agreements (RTAs). T/F

     Hint   Regional trade agreements are special agreements.

6.   The goal of a free-trade area (FTA) is to abolish work permits among its members. T/F

     Hint   An FTA is the first step in regional economic integration.

7.   Only adjoining countries tend to establish FTAs. T/F

     Hint   Similarities in political ideologies, culture, and language tend to attract.

8. Custom unions levy a common external tariff on goods being imported from nonmembers. T/F

    Hint Customs unions are the second stage of regional economic integration.

9. A common market builds on the base of a customs union and further allows free mobility of production factors. T/F

    Hint A common market is the third step in regional economic integration.

10. Trade creation allows consumers access to more goods at lower prices and is considered a major benefit of regional economic integration. T/F

    Hint Consider the concept of new trade opportunities for more efficient producers.

11. Trade diversion benefits the consumers with lowering prices and increasing choices. T/F

    Hint Trade diversion favors member countries over nonmember countries.

12. The Treaties of Rome established the European Coal and Steel Community (ECSC). T/F

    Hint The ECSC was established in 1951.

13. Austria, Finland, and Sweden became members of the European Union (EU) in 1995. T/F

    Hint Additional members were added in 1995 to bring the number of members to 15.

14. The European Parliament is comprised of two representatives from each member country. T/F

    Hint The European Parliament membership is based on each member country's population.

15. NAFTA members in the year 2000 include Canada, the United States, and Mexico. T/F

    Hint NAFTA means North American Free Trade Agreement.

MULTIPLE CHOICE

1. Ford's first foray into Europe was:

    Hint Ford sold its first export in the UK.

    a. in 1908, when it opened a sales branch in Paris.
    b. in 1925, when it established an assembly plant in Germany.
    c. in 1903, when Ford sold its first export in the UK.
    d. after WWII to compete with the Volkswagen.

2. Regional economic integration includes the following four basic types:

    Hint The four types develop in a progression.

    a. FTA, customs union, common union, and common market
    b. FTA, customs union, common market, and common currency.
    c. It is false to assume that there are four basic types of regional economic integration.
    d. FTA, customs union, common market, and complete economic integration to include a common currency and a degree of political integration.

3. Dynamic effects of integration occur when:

Hint   Consider the positive consequences of a reduction in trade barriers.

a. less-efficient producers have a competitive advantage.
b. trade barriers come down and the size of the market increases.
c. trade shifts to less-efficient producers.
d. trade is concentrated in a war zone.

4. An example of a Free Trade Association is:

Hint   Free Trade Associations are the first step in regional economic integration.

a. EFTA
b. EU
c. MERCOSUR
d. None of the examples is correct.

5. The Treaty of Maastricht was not easy to design because:

Hint   The Treaty of Maastricht sought a consensus among diverse political cultures.

a. member countries had different opinions regarding the role the EU should play in the member's national policies.
b. EFTA members refused to cooperate with EC members.
c. Switzerland dominated the meetings.
d. Both (a) and (c) are correct.

6. The EU countries that chose not to participate in the new euro in 1999 were:

Hint   Consider the countries that chose not to and the country that was not ready because it did not meet the monetary policy criteria, which was decided at Maastricht.

a. Britain, Sweden, Denmark, and Germany.
b. Britain, Sweden, Malta, and Greece.
c. Britain, Sweden, Denmark, and Greece.
d. All EU countries participated.

7. NAFTA has a number of different trade arrangements from what is commonly considered for an FTA because:

Hint   Consider the political clout of certain groups in North America.

a. Mexico insisted on stronger environmental policies.
b. labor unions and environmentalists strongly objected to the agreement.
c. Both (a) and (b) are correct.
d. civil rights groups worried about the possibility of Mexican labor being exploited for cheaper wages.

8. The disruption of the WTO meeting in Seattle in November of 1999 was largely caused by:

Hint   Consider the two major groups who were opposed to NAFTA.

a. terrorists objecting to U.S. policies in the Middle East.
b. civil rights demonstrators objecting to discrimination in Seattle housing.
c. Seattle transportation workers who wanted to disable the city traffic flow.
d. None of the above is correct.

9. APEC, the Asia Pacific Economic Cooperation, was formed to promote:

   Hint   APEC is comprised of 21 Pacific Rim countries.

   a.   protectionist measures and to follow union demands.
   b.   inward-looking regionalism as in the EU and NAFTA.
   c.   multilateral cooperation in trade and investment in the Pacific Rim areas.
   d.   APEC does not exist.

10. Commodity Agreements are no longer necessary now that regional economic integration dominates.

    Hint   Commodity agreements are concerned with price and supply stability.

    a.   No, commodity agreements continue between producing and exporting countries for commodities such as: crude petroleum, copper, coffee, etc.
    b.   Yes, commodity agreements are medieval and no longer necessary.
    c.   Yes, each regional economic trade area addresses commodities and therefore the old commodity agreements are not longer needed.
    d.   Commodity agreements are synonymous with Regional Economic Integration.

11. The Gulf War has been cited as an example of a consequence of disagreements among OPEC members regarding the pricing of oil.

    Hint   Kuwait was exceeding its production quota.

    a.   No, the Gulf War was a mere act of aggression.
    b.   Yes, a major reason for the invasion of Kuwait was in retaliation of Kuwait exceeding its production quota, as had been agreed on with other OPEC members.
    c.   No, OPEC member were not concerned about individual member countries exceeding their production quota.
    d.   The Gulf War should not be seen as a trade war.

12. Environmental issues are national in nature and therefore do not require cross-national agreements.

    Hint   Consider the implications of acid rain and whale hunting.

    a.   Yes, environmental issues are confined to national borders.
    b.   Yes, cross-national agreements target defense issues and resource issues and not environmental issues.
    c.   None of the answers is correct.
    d.   No, environmental issues are becoming increasingly important as global issues and often require cross-national agreements

13. Regional integration in Africa has accelerated.

    Hint   Africa has difficult political issues that make economic integration slow.

    a.   No, Africa's political and economic problems contributes to its slow pace in collaborating for regional economic integration.
    b.   Yes, Africa's economic integration process has been impressively fast.
    c.   Africa is too large a continent to consider for regional integration.
    d.   All of the above are false.

14. The Crystal Lake Manufacturing case clearly demonstrates that U.S. labor is less productive than Mexican labor.

   Hint   Consider all issues including substitution and wages.

   a.   Yes, Mexican broom workers showed that brooms can be produced most efficiently in Mexico.
   b.   Yes, President Clinton made it clear that U.S. broom workers were not working hard enough.
   c.   The Crystal Lake Manufacturing case shows the complexity of an industry that was challenged with cheaper labor with the NAFTA arena and also challenged by substitutes for its product line.
   d.   The broom case shows that environmental issues play an important part in the broom industry.

15. Trade issues and environmental issues are interrelated in that:

   Hint   Countries with strong economies can afford to spend money to address environmental issues.

   a.   studies show that countries with low income levels cannot spend much money to clean up the environment.
   b.   trade issues are completely separate from environmental issues.
   c.   the wealthier the country, the less its people are about environmental issues.
   d.   None of the answers is correct.

INTERNET EXERCISES

Exercise 1.
Ford Motor Company
http://www.ford.com/
Visit the Ford Motor Company Web site and browse the Ford products. Then, visit at least five different Ford Motor Company sites by clicking on Global Websites. Where are these sites and are they within a regional economic trades area? If so, which ones? Consider why Ford is located in these areas. Relate your reasoning to Chapter 7. How large are the markets in the economically integrated areas? What are the benefits to Ford? Discuss.

Exercise 2.
European Union
http://europa.eu.int/index-en.htm
Visit the EU Web site and explore the section headed Institutions by going to at least five different home pages of the institutions. Institution home pages worth exploring are: Parliament, Commission, Court of Justice, European Central Bank, etc. Give a brief overview of each institution home page Web site and summarize by showing the overall relationship these sites have to the EU.

Exercise 3.
NAFTA
http://www.mexico-trade.com/nafta.html
Visit the NAFTA information Web site and explore at least five links at this site. Write a brief overview of each link and discuss how this site pertains to the discussions in Chapter 7.

Exercise 4.
MERCOSUR
http://www.americasnet.com/mauritz/mercosur/english/
Visit the MERCOSUR Web site and note the map that shows the MERCOSUR members. Explore a minimum of five links on this Web site and compare this information to the EU and NAFTA Web sites. How are they similar? How do they differ? Describe your findings in a brief essay.

Exercise 5.
OPEC
http://www.opec.org/members.htm
Visit the OPEC Web site. Note the members and click on each member country to assess its petroleum reserves and production capacity. Click on the Web sites of the various national oil companies and compare them. How do they differ? How are they the same? Visit the "history" link and note the first members to those now. Write an essay discussing this Web site by giving an historical overview of OPEC and its members. Relate this Web site to the section titled "Commodity Agreements" in the text.

CHAPTER 7 ANSWER KEY

True/False

1. False   Yes, it is false to assume the Ford did not recognize the common market potential of Europe. Ford was among the leaders in changing its management structure to include its European operations under one regional umbrella organization known as Ford Europe Incorporated.
    Difficulty: easy
    Topic: Case: Ford Europe

2. True   Yes, the United States in some respects is a perfect example of economic integration in that all 50 states share a common currency and factor mobility.
    Difficulty: easy
    Topic: Introduction

3. True   Yes, regionally integrated countries share preferential status among its members
    Difficulty: moderate
    Topic: Introduction

4. False   On the contrary, regional trading groups are an important influence on MNEs' strategies.
    Difficulty: moderate
    Topic: Introduction

5. True   Yes, nearly all of the WTO members have concluded regional trade agreements with other countries.
    Difficulty: moderate
    Topic: Introduction

6. False   It is false to assume that free migration of labor is a high priority in the initial step of creating a free-trade area.
    Difficulty: moderate
    Topic: Regional Economic Integration

7. False   Yes, although neighboring countries tend to ally themselves in FTAs, other similarities such as political ideologies are strong forces for FTAs.
    Difficulty: moderate
    Topic: Regional Economic Integration

8. True   Yes, in addition to eliminating internal tariffs, member countries levy a common external tariff.
    Difficulty: easy
    Topic: Regional Economic Integration

9. True   Yes, free mobility of labor and capital in addition to the FTA and customs union privileges are part of the conditions a common market establishes for its members.
    Difficulty: hard
    Topic: Regional Economic Integration

10. True   Yes, trade creation is a concept that implies that more-efficient producers among member countries can now compete on equitable terms with less-efficient producers and thereby give consumers choices in purchasing the cheapest goods.
    Difficulty: hard
    Topic: The Effects of Integration

11. False Yes, it is false to assume that trade diversion benefits a country's consumers. On the contrary, trade diversion shifts trade to member countries even though companies in nonmember countries may be more efficient. If this is the case, then the consumer will likely pay a higher price for the less efficiently produced goods.
Difficulty: hard
Topic: The Effects of Integration

12. False Yes, it is false to assume that the Treaties of Rome established the ECSC. Instead, it was the Treaty of Paris, signed in 1951, that established the ECSC.
Difficulty: moderate
Topic: European Union Milestones

13. True Yes, Austria, Finland, and Sweden became the 13th, 14th, and 15th members of the EU in 1995.
Difficulty: easy
Topic: European Union Milestones

14. False It is false to assume that the European Parliament has equal representation from each member country. Instead, the Parliament members represent population bases from their home countries and range widely. An example is: Germany has 99 members and Luxembourg 6.
Difficulty: hard
Topic: The European Parliament

15. True Yes, in the year 2000, the NAFTA members are Canada, Mexico, and the United States.
Difficulty: easy
Topic: North American Free Trade Agreement (NAFTA)

Multiple Choice

1. c. Yes, this event is considered Ford's first foray in Europe.
Difficulty: easy
Topic: Case: Ford in Europe—an Historical Overview

2. d. Yes, these are the four basic types of regional economic integration.
Difficulty: moderate
Topic: Regional Economic Integration

3. b. Yes, this example shows the dynamic growth potential a reduction in trade barriers can have on an integrated market.
Difficulty: hard
Topic: The Effects of Integration

4. a. Yes, EFTA is the European Free Trade Association.
Difficulty: easy
Topic: Major Regional Trading Groups

5. a. Yes, the negotiations at Maastricht considered issues on political union and monetary union, which brought up many differences among the members.
Difficulty: easy
Topic: The Treaty of Maastricht

6. c. Yes, Britain, Sweden, and Denmark choose not to participate in the new euro and Greece was not yet ready to participate.
Difficulty: moderate.
Topic: The Euro

7. b.   Yes, labor unions in Canada and the United States feared the cheaper labor in competing with higher wages in their countries and environmentalists in both Canada and the United States were concerned about Mexico's lax environmental laws.
    Difficulty: moderate.
    Topic: North American Free Trade Agreement (NAFTA)

8. d.   Yes, none of the above responses addresses the main issues, which were concerns by labor and environmental groups who worried about Mexico's cheap labor and lax environmental laws.
    Difficulty: moderate.
    Topic: Special Provisions of NAFTA

9. c.   Yes, APEC's concern is over regional economic integration and was formed to keep trade liberalized.
    Difficulty: moderate
    Topic: Other Regional Economic Groups in Latin America, Asia, and Africa

10. a.   Yes, an example of producer alliances is: OPEC (petroleum products) and ICCO, cocoa products.
    Difficulty: moderate
    Topic: Commodity Agreements

11. b.   Yes, Sadam Hussein justified his invasion of Kuwait by stating he wanted to gain control over Kuwait's oil supplies.
    Difficulty: hard
    Topic: The Organization of Petroleum Exporting Countries (OPEC)

12. d.   Yes, trade issues and environmental issues are often closely intertwined, and cross-national agreements are one method of addressing these concerns.
    Difficulty: hard
    Topic: The Environment

13. a.   Yes, Africa's internal national conflicts do not lend themselves to a rapid regional economic integration process.
    Difficulty: moderate.
    Topic: Looking to the Future

14. c.   Yes, the broom case reveals the internal concerns with unemployment one industry faced with the new trade agreements as well as with other competitive industry factors.
    Difficulty: hard
    Topic: Industry Response

15. a.   Yes, one of the arguments in the NAFTA controversy regarding Mexico's poor environmental laws was that Mexico would benefit from NAFTA economically and thus naturally strengthen its environmental standards with these enhanced economic resources.
    Difficulty: moderate
    Topic: Ethical Dilemmas and Social Responsibility

Chapter 8

Foreign Direct Investment

CHAPTER OBJECTIVES

1. To explain why investors and governments view direct investments differently than portfolio investments.

2. To demonstrate how companies acquire foreign direct investments.

3. To evaluate the relationship between foreign trade and international factors mobility, especially direct investment.

4. To classify companies' motivations for foreign direct investment.

5. To explain companies' advantages from foreign direct investments.

6. To show the major global patterns of foreign direct investment.

TRUE/FALSE

1. The Bridgestone Tire Company expanded to the United States largely because of the OEM potential in tires.

    Hint   Bridgestone Tire Company originated in Japan.

2. Bridgestone's purchase of Firestone's automobile tire operation is an example of an ineffective FDI.

    Hint   Bridgestone gained a significant market share in supplying Ford and GM in North America and parts of Europe and South America.

3. U.S. government restrictions on imported tires were a major reason for Bridgestone's FDI.

    Hint   The U.S. government imposed restrictions on tire imports.

4. Government authorities worry that FDIs can impact their countries negatively.

    Hint   FDIs can have a significant impact on a country's economy.

5. A direct investment is not the same as a portfolio investment.

    Hint   Control accompanies direct investments.

6. Only if a company has a 100% share in a foreign direct investment is it assured full control.

    Hint   Control in a foreign direct investment is not clear-cut.

7. The appropriability theory assumes that FDIs will collaborate with their competitors in the host country.

    Hint   The appropriability theory cautions against rivalry and access to joint resources.

8. Internalization within the context of FDI means that a company chooses to operate its foreign holdings rather than transferring technology or use other intermediaries to establish itself in a foreign market.

    Hint   The Concern about Control.

9. Availability is not an issue in FDI buy versus build decisions.

    Hint   A company may buy or construct a new facility.

10. FDI plays an insignificant role in factor movements.

    Hint   Factor movement is an alternative to trade.

11. Pressure exists for the most abundant factors to move to countries with greater scarcity—where they can command better return.

    Hint   Factor proportions may vary widely among countries.

12. Many exports would not occur if overseas investments did not exist.

    Hint   A company may export capital equipment when building a facility abroad.

13. One of the three major reasons for FDIs is to acquire resources.

    Hint   Companies may set up foreign production for labor-intensive industries in countries with abundant and cheap labor.

14. Transportation costs are not considered in an FDI decision because transportation costs are simply added to the cost of a good.

    Hint   Costs are key to competitive factors.

15. All scale economies benefit by moving plants to cheap labor areas.

    Hint   Retooling for foreign markets may need to take place.

MULTIPLE CHOICE

1. Although Bridgestone Tire concentrated most of its efforts on its home market in Asia until the mid-1980s, the foreign sales also grew mainly because:

    Hint Japan car exports increased during this time period.

    a.   of Firestone's direct tires purchases from Bridgestone.
    b.   of the scarcity of raw materials in other parts of the world.
    c.   of the original equipment market (OEM).
    d.   Bridgestone's tires were not exported until the 1990s.

2. In an effort to establish a manufacturing presence in the early 1980s in the United States, Bridgestone:

    Hint Bridgestone committed to a FDI in 1982 in the United States.

    a.   bought a truck-tire plant from Firestone in 1982.
    b.   bought Firestone's automobile tire operation in 1980.
    c.   bought the Michelin dealerships in the United States in the mid 1980s.
    d.   did not care to establish a market in the United States.

3. The amount of ownership necessary for companies to control their foreign operations is:

Hint A number of factors need to be considered with regard to control and include political considerations.

    a.   51% ownership is sufficient to maintain control of a foreign investment.

    b.   although the amount of ownership plays a role in how much a foreign operation may have, the overall control is more complicated because of potential governmental interferences and therefore the answer is not clear-cut.

    c.   minimal if the existing government has approved the operation.

    d.   FDIs do not have control over their operations.

4. Control is important to foreign companies because:

Hint Consider the various risks to company resources such as capital, patents, trademarks and management know-how.

    a.   without control, others can use the company resources to undermine the competitive position of the foreign company.

    b.   the company would suffer from image problems if it did not appear controlling to foreigners.

    c.   it is mandated by shareholders.

    d.   home governments take care of control issues for FDIs, and these are not problematic.

5. Although most FDI requires some type of international capital movement, an investor may transfer other types of assets such as:

Hint Assets include tangible and intangible assets.

    a.   only capital assets are transferred with FDI investments no more.

    b.   capital and management know-how are the only two assets an FDI may transfer to conform to home-government regulations.

    c.   it is not correct to assume that FDIs require international capital movements.

    d.   management know-how, control systems, patents, and trademarks are some of the additional assets a company may transfer with an FDI.

6. The only way companies can invest in a foreign country is to acquire an interest in an existing operation.

Hint Consider the buy-versus-build decision.

    a.   Yes, buying an existing business is the only way to invest in a foreign country.

    b.   It is not possible to buy a business in a foreign country.

    c.   Acquiring an interest in an existing business in a foreign country is only one way to invest; the other way is to build a business.

    d.   None of the above is correct.

7. When companies move abroad to produce basically the same products they produce at home, their direct investments are:

Hint Consider this from the perspective of a lateral move.

    a.   vertically integrated.

    b.   horizontal expansion.

    c.   at the end of the product life cycle.

    d.   Companies would not duplicate production from home-country production.

8. One important reason companies choose to produce in a foreign country is:

    Hint Consider trade restrictions.

    a. key managers may have strong preferences to live in that country.
    b. trade restrictions made it difficult to import their products into the country or economic region.
    c. religious traditions in the foreign country may be appealing to the spiritual values of top managers.
    d. the country may have a well-organized union for their particular industry.

9. If a company controls different stages of making its product such as from raw materials through to its final distribution, this is called:

    Hint Picture the line of progression in this process.

    a. good business.
    b. breaking antitrust laws.
    c. horizontal integration.
    d. vertical integration.

10. Some companies produce different components or different portions of their product line in different parts of the world to take advantage of low labor costs, capital, and raw materials. This is called:

    Hint Consider the rationale and selection process.

    a. just-in-time manufacturing systems (JIT).
    b. horizontal expansion.
    c. the product life cycle theory.
    d. rationalized production.

11. The example given of Johnson Controls, a U.S. manufacturer that expanded into Europe, shows this company's efforts to:

    Hint Diversifying locations can cushion risk.

    a. minimize its exposure to cyclical economic downturns in the United States.
    b. become vertically integrated.
    c. minimize labor costs.
    d. None of the answers is correct.

12. The Chinese National Petroleum Corporation's strategy to invest in Kazakhstan, Peru, the Sudan, and Venezuela oil production is an example of:

    Hint Consider that the Chinese government owns the Chinese National Petroleum Corporation.

    a. following customers.
    b. a political motive on the part of China to reduce the risk of dependence on foreign companies for its oil supply.
    c. The statement is not correct. The Chinese do not invest in foreign oil production.
    d. Both (a) and (b) are correct.

13. The largest investors in the United States in 1998 were:

    Hint Consider the two strong island economies in the world.

    a. Malta and Australia.
    b. The United States does not allow foreign companies to invest within the United States.
    c. the United Kingdom and Japan.
    d. Cuba and Libya.

14. FDI sometimes has chain effects because:

    Hint Consider the interrelationships with vendors.

    a. when one company makes an investment, some of its suppliers may follow with investments of their own.
    b. the chain of political payoffs is part of FDI.
    c. Both (a) and (b) are correct.
    d. None of the answers is correct.

15. What are the key factors that influenced the FDI decision for Cran Chile?

    Hint Consider the growing conditions necessary for cranberries.

    a. Cran Chile represents a "following market" decision.
    b. The key factor to grow cranberries in Chile is reduced transportation costs.
    c. Nationalism
    d. Resource seeking

INTERNET EXERCISES

Exercise 1.
Bridgestone Tire Company
http://www.bridgestone-firestone.com
Familiarize yourself with the Bridgestone Web site. Consider the locations and product lines for this Japanese based company. Reflect on the Bridgestone case and discuss how Bridgestone's FDI has changed since the early 1980s.

Exercise 2.
Electrolux
http://www.electrolux.com
Visit the Electrolux Group Web site. What are the history and the home country of this company? Who are the customers? Discuss scale economies in relation of this company's product line.

Exercise 3.
BP Amoco
http://www.bpamoco.com
Consider the BP Amoco Web site and explore the information on the company and its products. Discuss if this company is vertically or horizontally integrated. Be specific.

Exercise 4.
Mercedes-Benz
http://www.mbusa.com
Visit the Mercedes-Benz Web site. Familiarize yourself with the company and its products and then discuss the concept of rationalized production as it pertains to this company.

Exercise 5.

OECD

http://www.oecd.org/search/first.htm

Visit the OECD Web site and familiarize yourself with at least six OECD activities that relate to FDI. Give a brief overview of each activity and provide an overview of OECD as an organization.

CHAPTER 8 ANSWER KEY

True/False

1. True   Yes, Bridgestone Tire Company was concerned to continue to supply Japanese automakers that were
            opening plants in the United States.
    Difficulty: moderate
    Topic: Case: Bridgestone Tire Company

2. False   Bridgestone's investment in Firestone was an effective FDI strategy because it provided access to
            Firestone accounts in North and South America as well as Europe.
    Difficulty: easy
    Topic: Case: Bridgestone Tire Company

3. True   Yes, because of restrictive U.S. tariffs on imported tires to the United States. Bridgestone opted to
            manufacture tires within the United States instead.
    Difficulty: hard
    Topic: Case: Bridgestone Tire Company

4. True   Yes, foreign direct investments are a worry to many government authorities because an outsider's
            control of a company can lead to decisions contrary to their country's best interest.
    Difficulty: moderate
    Topic: The Meaning of Foreign Direct Investment

5. True   Yes, portfolio investments do not required control.
    Difficulty: hard
    Topic: The Meaning of Foreign Direct Investment

6. False   Yes, it is false to assume that a company may have total control even over a 100% ownership if the
            foreign government chooses to exercise control over the company.
    Difficulty: hard
    Topic: The Meaning of Foreign Direct Investment

7. False   Yes, it is not correct to state that collaboration for mutual benefit is assumed in the appropriability
            theory.
    Difficulty: hard
    Topic: The Concern about Control

8. True   Yes, internalization means a company chooses control through the self-handling of operations in a
            foreign country.
    Difficulty: hard
    Topic: The Concern about Control

9. False   Yes, it is false to assume that availability is not an issue in a company's decision whether to buy or
            build.
    Difficulty: easy
    Topic: Buy-versus-Build Decision

10. False   Yes, it is false to assume that factor movements are not a significant reason for FDIs.
    Difficulty: hard
    Topic: The Relationship of Trade and Factor Mobility

11. True   Yes, in countries where labor is abundant, laborers tend to go to countries, if permitted, where they
            get higher wages.
    Difficulty: moderate
    Topic: The Relationship of Trade and Factor Mobility

12. True   Yes, FDIs tend to export home-country products and services to their foreign locations.
   Difficulty: moderate
   Topic: Complementarities of Trade and Direct Investment

13. True   Yes, resources such as cheap or skilled labor may be one reason for companies to move to another country that has these in abundance.
   Difficulty: moderate
   Topic: Relationship of FDI to Companies' Objectives

14. False   Yes, transportation costs do play a key role in determining a company's competitiveness, as was the case with Bridgestone.
   Difficulty: moderate
   Topic: FDI Motivations to Achieve Sales Expansion

15. False   Yes, is not correct to assume that all scale economies can benefit by moving abroad. Other considerations such as retooling for foreign markets must also be addressed.
   Difficulty: hard
   Topic: FDI Motivations to Achieve Sales Expansion

Multiple Choice

1. c.   Yes, the OEM contributed to Bridgestone's success in foreign markets because Japanese carmakers used Bridgestone tires for their cars, which when exported, contributed to Bridgestone's export market.
   Difficulty: moderate
   Topic: Case: Bridgestone Tire Company

2. a.   Yes, with this initial Firestone plant, Bridgestone was able to penetrate the U.S. market to have 10% of the new car market for tires by 1987.
   Difficulty: easy
   Topic: Case: Bridgestone Tire Company

3. b.   Yes, many factors can influence the amount of control a foreign operation may have and this needs to be determined on a case-by-case basis.
   Difficulty: moderate
   Topic: The Meaning of Foreign Direct Investment

4. a.   Yes, it is true that control minimizes risks for a company whereas if the company transferred vital resources such as patents and trademarks, it would make itself more vulnerable to competitors.
   Difficulty: moderate
   Topic: The Concern about Control

5. d.   Yes, in addition to capital transfers other, intangible assets such as management skills and registered trademarks may also be included.
   Difficulty: hard
   Topic: Methods of Acquisition

6. c.   Yes, one way to invest in another country is to buy an existing business. Another way also is to build a new venture in the foreign country.
   Difficulty: moderate
   Topic: Buy-versus-Build Decision

7. b. Yes, this is an example of a horizontal expansion.
Difficulty: hard
Topic: FDI Motivations to Achieve Sales Expansion

8. b. Yes, a key reason for companies to move production to lucrative markets is that government-imposed trade restrictions may make it too difficult to import into these markets. Consider the example of the EU.
Difficulty: moderate
Topic: Trade Restrictions

9. d. Yes, a company is considered vertically integrated if it owns the progressive chain of productions such as: a cattle ranch, meat packing plant, restaurant.
Difficulty: moderate
Topic: FDI Motivations to Acquire Resources

10. d. Yes, rationalized production describes the process of selecting the most advantages sources for producing various components of different portions of their product line.
Difficulty: hard
Topic: FDI Motivations to Acquire Resources

11. a. Yes, this is an example of a company's efforts to minimize risks from cyclical downturns by establishing a buffer base.
Difficulty: hard
Topic: Risk Minimization Objectives

12. b. Yes, the Chinese National Petroleum Corporation is a Chinese government-owned company that invested in foreign oil production to minimize the risk of becoming dependent on foreign companies for its oil supply.
Difficulty: moderate
Topic: Political Motives

13. c. Yes, the U.K. and Japan investments in the United States in 1998 accounted for about 19 and 16%, respectively, of FDI there.
Difficulty: moderate
Topic: Location of Investment

14. a. Yes, FDI may produce a chain reaction as series of dependent suppliers follow the first company's lead.
Difficulty: moderate
Topic: Summary.

15. d. Yes, the Chile site offered land and labor conducive for cranberry growing. The most significant factor was obtaining land that was no longer easily available in the United States because of wetland protection laws.
Difficulty: moderate easy hard
Topic: Case: Cran Chile

Chapter 9

The Foreign Exchange Market

CHAPTER OBJECTIVES

1.   To learn the fundamentals of foreign exchange.

2.   To identify the major characteristics of the foreign exchange market and how governments control the flow of currencies across national borders.

3.   To understand why companies deal in foreign exchange.

4.   To describe how the foreign exchange market works.

5.   To examine the different institutions that deal in foreign exchange.

TRUE/FALSE

1.   Foreign exchange can be in many different forms.

      Hint   Foreign exchange is money denominated in the currency of another nation or group of nations.

2.   An exchange rate is the price of a currency.

      Hint   Currencies are valued according to the exchange rate.

3.   The foreign exchange market is controlled by the buyers.

      Hint   Foreign exchange is determined by transactions.

4.   One segment of the foreign exchange market is called OTC.

      Hint   OTC markets are comprised of financial institutions.

5.   Exchange-trade options and futures are part of the OTC segment.

      Hint   Foreign exchange instruments are traded at securities exchanges such as the Philadelphia Stock Exchange.

6.   Options are the obligation to trade foreign currency in the future.

      Hint   Options connote choice.

7.   Futures contracts are the same as options.

      Hint   Contracts are binding.

8.   The Bank of International Settlements (BIS) based in Basel, Switzerland, is a branch of the World Bank.

      Hint   BIS provides specialized services.

9.   In the spot market, the spread is the difference between the bid and offer rates.

      Hint   The spread is the trader's profit margin.

10.   Foreign currencies fluctuate daily.

Hint   Many factors impinge on currency rates.

11.   Hard currencies are represented by silver or gold coins rather than paper money.

Hint   Hard currencies stands for strength.

12.   The purchase of foreign currency on one market for immediate resale on another market for quick profit is called arbitrage.

Hint   Consider that root word arbitrate which means "quick judgment."

13.   Exotic currencies are currencies received in the illicit global pornographic market.

Hint   Exotic currencies allow banks to develop niche markets.

14.   The Philadelphia Stock Exchange (PHLX) is the only exchange in the United States that trades foreign currency options.

Hint   The PHLX offers standardized and customized options.

15.   A cross rate is the fee added when currencies cross international borders.

Hint   Consider nondollar currency exchanges.

MULTIPLE CHOICE

1.   The OTC market is comprised of:

Hint   The OTC markets deal with most foreign exchange activity.

    a.   the Philadelphia Stock Exchange and commercial banks.
    b.   investment banks and the Chicago Mercantile Exchange.
    c.   both commercial banks and investment banks.
    d.   None of the above is correct.

2.   Spot transactions involve the exchange of currency:

Hint   Spot transactions have an element of immediacy.

    a.   on the spot and within the hour.
    b.   the second day after the date on which two foreign exchange traders agree to the transaction.
    c.   in a black market situation.
    d.   Spot rates no longer exist.

3. A futures contract is:

Hint   Consider the need to secure foreign currency for a specific payment date in the future.

   a.   a contract for exclusive currency transactions in the future.
   b. an agreement between two parties to buy or sell a particular currency at a particular price on a particular future date.
   c.   Both (a) and (b) are correct.
   d.   None of the above is correct.

4. The U.S. dollar is the most important currency in the foreign exchange market because:

Hint   Consider the volume of US dollars traded globally.

   a.   it comprises one side of 87 percent of all foreign currency transactions worldwide.
   b.   the Deutsche mark is no longer a viable trading currency.
   c.   the U.S. dollar is not the most important currency, it is merely an important currency.
   d.   None of the above is correct.

5. Currencies that are not fully convertible are often called:

Hint   If not fully convertible, then a currency is less desirable.

   a.   hard currencies.
   b.   All currencies are fully convertible.
   c.   Eurodollars.
   d.   soft currencies or weak currencies.

6. To conserve scarce foreign exchange, governments may resort to:

Hint   Governments may impose restrictions on companies or individuals who want to exchange money.

   a.   It is not a function of government to control foreign exchange.
   b.   All governments resort to a multiple exchange-rate system.
   c.   import licensing, multiple exchange rates, import deposit requirements, and quantity controls.
   d.   black market activity.

7. Quantity controls in foreign exchange tend to directly impact:

Hint   Quantity controls on foreign exchange limit the amount of money a person can convert to a foreign currency.

   a.   Governments do not resort to quantity controls in foreign exchange.
   b.   exporters of the country where the quantity controls are implemented.
   c.   tourists and importers.
   d.   Both (b) and (c) are correct.

8. Speculation is the buying or selling of a foreign currency that:

Hint   Consider that speculation is a two-sided issue.

   a.   assures a quick profit.
   b.   is too risky and no longer practiced.
   c.   is a high-risk activity with little chance of profit.
   d.   has both an element of risk and the chance of great profit.

9.   The BIS estimates there are about _____ dealer institutions worldwide.

      Hint   Dealer institutions are the intermediaries for smaller banks for foreign exchange.

      a.   Each country has only one central dealer institute.
      b.   2,000 dealer
      c.   The BIS does not perform these types of estimates.
      d.   200

10.   Nicholas Leeson's ability to incur losses in excess of $1 billion dollars for Barings PLC shows:

      Hint   Consider control systems for speculative activities.

      a.   a lack of checks and balances within the Barings bank.
      b.   luck is important in trading securities internationally.
      c.   the power of the Singapore government to interfere with securities trading.
      d.   that very young traders are incompetent.

INTERNET EXERCISES

Exercise 1.
Bank of International Settlements
http://www.bis.org
Go to the Bank of International Settlements (BIS) Web site and note the member central banks. Click on and study at least six member banks to gain an understanding of the relationship between the BIS and the member banks. Discuss your findings

Exercise 2.
Bank of International Settlements
http://www.bis.org
Go to the BIS Web site and click on "Why the BIS was founded." Then investigate other areas of interest on the BIS site. Write a brief essay on the BIS and its functions.

Exercise 3.
Universal Currency Converter and Rubicon
http://www.xe.net/ucc/
http://www.rubicon.com/passport/currency/ccfram.htm
Describe the services and activities of these Web sites and how they relate to the introduction of Chapter 9.

Exercise 4.
FTSE
http://www.ft-se.co.uk/
Relate this Web site to the discussion on securities trading in Chapter 9.

Exercise 5.
Report to the Board of Banking
http://newrisk.ifci.ch/introduction.htm
Access the Case Studies for further study. Discuss the additional insights regarding the Barings bank dilemma found on this site.

CHAPTER 9 ANSWER KEY

True/False

1. True   Yes, foreign exchange can be in the form of cash, credit or debit cards funds, traveler's checks, bank deposits, or other short-term claims.
   Difficulty: easy
   Topic: Introduction

2. True   Yes, the number of units of one currency that buys one unit of another currency is the exchange rate.
   Difficulty: easy
   Topic: Introduction

3. False   Yes, it is not correct to assume that buyers of foreign exchange control the market. Both buyers and sellers can strongly influence the exchange rate.
   Difficulty: moderate
   Topic: Introduction

4. True   Yes, the over-the-counter market (OTC) is one of the major segments of the foreign exchange market.
   Difficulty: moderate
   Topic: Major Characteristics of the Foreign Exchange Market

5. False   Yes, OTC markets provide different functions from the exchange-trade markets that trade foreign exchange instruments such as exchange-trade options and futures.
   Difficulty: hard
   Topic: Major Characteristics of the Foreign Exchange Market

6. False   Yes, it is false to assume that options are obligations when they are in fact rights to trade a foreign currency in the future.
   Difficulty: moderate
   Topic: Brief Description of Foreign Exchange Instruments

7. False   Yes, a futures contract is an agreement between two parties to buy or sell a particular currency at a particular price on a particular future date.
   Difficulty: hard
   Topic: Brief Description of Foreign Exchange Instruments

8. False   Yes, it is false to assume that BIS is a branch of the World Bank even though it does provide specific services to central banks around the world.
   Difficulty: moderate
   Topic: The Size, Composition, and Location of the Foreign Exchange Market.

9. True   Yes, the spread in the spot market is that portion between the buy and sell rate that is also the profit for the trader.
   Difficulty: moderate
   Topic: Major Foreign Exchange Instruments

10. True   Yes, it is true that currencies fluctuate daily and a manager involved in international trade should monitor these fluctuations on a regular basis.
    Difficulty: easy
    Topic: Major Foreign Exchange Instruments.

11. False   Yes, it is false to refer to gold and silver coins as hard currencies when referring to the foreign exchange market.
Difficulty: easy
Topic: Foreign Exchange Convertibility

12. True   Yes, arbitrage is a speculative activity that currency traders engage in for quick profit.
Difficulty: moderate
Topic: How Companies Use Foreign Exchange

13. False   Yes it is false to assume that exotic currencies are related to a global pornographic market. Instead, exotic currencies represent unusual currencies such as the Russian ruble or Mexican peso because they tend to be associated with higher risk.
Difficulty: moderate
Topic: Commercial and Investment Banks.

14. True   Yes, the PHLX lists eight dollar-based and two cross-rate standardized currency options contracts, which settle in the actual physical currency.
Difficulty: hard
Topic: The Philadelphia Stock Exchange

15. False   Yes, it is false to state that cross rates represent fees. A cross rate is the exchange rate between two nondollar currencies.
Difficulty: moderate
Topic: Summary

Multiple Choice

1. c.   Yes, the OTC market is comprised of institutions like Bank of America and Merrill-Lynch.
Difficulty: moderate
Topic: Major Characteristics of the Foreign Exchange Market

2. b.   Yes, that is correct, and in addition, the rate at which the transaction is settled is the spot rate.
Difficulty: moderate
Topic: Major Characteristics of the Foreign Exchange Market

3. b.   Yes, the specificity stated above describes a futures contract.
Difficulty: moderate
Topic: Brief Description of Foreign Exchange Instruments

4. a.   Yes, according to the Bank of International Settlements, the U.S. dollar is traded as the most favored currency worldwide.
Difficulty: easy
Topic: The Size, Composition, and Location of the Foreign Exchange Market

5. d.   Yes, soft, or weak, currencies tend to be less convertible that hard currencies and therefore are more risky to trade.
Difficulty: moderate
Topic: Foreign Exchange Convertibility

6. c.   Yes, these are among the measures that governments may use to conserve scarce foreign exchange.
Difficulty: hard
Topic: Foreign Exchange Convertibility

7.   c.   Yes, quantity controls limit the amount of foreign currency a local resident can purchase.

Difficulty: moderate

Topic: Foreign Exchange Convertibility

8.   d.   Yes, speculating in foreign currencies can generate good profits, but risks in doing so need to be carefully considered.

Difficulty: hard

Topic: How Companies Use Foreign Exchange

9.   b.   Yes, BIS estimates that there are about 2,000 dealer institutes worldwide, and of these, about 100–200 are market-making bands that are willing to quote bid and offer rates to anyone in the currency or currencies in which they deal.

Difficulty: easy

Topic: The Foreign Exchange Process

10.   a.   Yes, the lack of proper check and balances has been identified as the major reason for Leeson's ability to engage in ruthless speculation.

Difficulty: moderate

Topic: Ethical Dilemmas and Social Responsibility

Chapter 10

The Determination of Exchange Rates

CHAPTER OBJECTIVES

1. To describe the International Monetary Fund and its role in the determination of exchange rates.

2. To discuss the major exchange-rate arrangements countries use.

3. To identify the major determinants of exchange rates in the spot and forward markets.

4. To show how managers try to forecast exchange-rate movements using factors such as balance-of-payments statistics.

5. To explain how exchange-rate movements influence business decisions.

TRUE/FALSE

1. China's government created a new exchange system that would thereby eliminate a black market.

   Hint   Black markets tend to exist underground.

2. The International Monetary Fund (IMF) was the direct result of the Treaty of Versailles after WWI.

   Hint   The IMF sought to enhance economic stability to the post-WWII world.

3. The Bretton Woods Agreement established a system of fixed exchange rates.

   Hint   Each IMF member country set a par value for its currency based on gold and the U.S. dollar.

4. To help increase international reserves, the IMF created the Special Drawing Right (SDR)

   Hint   The SDR is an international reserve asset.

5. The Jamaica agreement of 1976 reiterated and enforced the concept of par values in exchange rates.

   Hint   The IMF had to change its rules in 1970 to accommodate floating exchange rates.

6. The IMF consults annually with countries to see if they are acting openly and responsibly in their exchange rate policies.

   Hint   The IMF has a surveillance program for exchange rates.

7. The New York Fed is responsible for intervening—for the United States—in foreign exchange markets to achieve dollar exchange-rate policy objectives.

   Hint   Each country has a central bank that is responsible for the policy affecting the value of its currency.

8. The degree to which a central bank actively manages its reserves to earn a profit is standardized for all countries.

   Hint   Each country is different and has its own priorities.

9. Currencies that float freely are controlled by the country's government.

   Hint Free connotes supply and demand

10. The bridge from interest rates to exchange rates can be explained by the International Fisher Effect (IFE).

    Hint The IFE theory holds that interest-rate differential is an unbiased predictor of future changes in the spot exchange rate.

MULTIPLE CHOICE

1. China's currency policy has been:

   Hint China has been reforming its banking system so that it could gain better access to foreign capital.

   a. locked in since 1949.
   b. to adjust to market conditions by changing from a dual-track foreign exchange-system to allow its currency to float according to market forces and then tried an experiment by pegging its currency to the U.S. dollar.
   c. to peg the RMB to the Japanese yen.
   d. effective in eliminating a black market for foreign exchange.

2. In foreign exchange, crawling peg rates have the following characteristics:

   Hint Costa Rica and Turkey use this method.

   a. The country pegs its currency at a fixed rate to a major currency or basket of currencies where the exchange rate fluctuates within a narrow margin of at most +/- 1 percent around a central rate.
   b. The currency is maintained within certain fluctuation margins around a central rate that is adjusted periodically at a fixed preannounced rate or in response to changes in selective quantity indicators.
   c. The currency is adjusted periodically in small amounts at a fixed, preannounced rate or in response to changes in selective quantitative indicators.
   d. None of the above is correct.

3. Black markets that deal in foreign exchange are more likely to thrive in:

   Hint A black market exists when people are willing to pay more for dollars than the official rate.

   a. countries with inflexible exchange-rate arrangements.
   b. when a currency is allowed to float.
   c. Black currency markets do not exist.
   d. None of the above is correct.

4. Central banks can intervene in currency markets by:

   Hint The intervention may depend on present market conditions.

   a. using a number of methods that are appropriate for that time and may include: coordination with other central banks, calling for reassurance to calm markets intervening, and resisting or supporting markets trends.
   b. Central banks are not concerned with currency markets.
   c. calling an election.
   d. Both (a) and (c) are correct.

5.   Currencies that float freely, respond to:

Hint   Consider the concept of laissez-faire.

a.   Currencies do not float freely.
b.   demand rather than supply.
c.   supply rather than demand.
d.   supply and demand conditions free from government interventions.

6.   Purchasing-power parity (PPP) claims that:

Hint   PPP is a well-known theory that seeks to define relationships between currencies.

a.   a change in relative inflation between two countries causes a major discrepancy in the prices of goods between these two countries.
b.   inflation leads to a reduction in the purchase of Big Macs.
c.   change in relative inflation between two countries must cause a change in exchange rates to keep the prices of goods in two countries fairly similar.
d.   Both (b) and (c) are correct.

7.   The two approaches managers can use to forecast exchange rates are:

Hint   Consider economic trends and exchange-rate trends.

a.   by contacting their local banks or trading companies.
b.   the fundamental and technical approach.
c.   Exchange rates are too unpredictable to forecast.
d.   caution and luck.

8.   Exchange rates are important factors for company strategies because:

Hint   Exchange rates affect price.

a.   they affect expenses when executives travel abroad.
b.   they have a significant impact on a company's strategy.
c.   Exchange rates play a minimal role for a domestic company.
d.   Both (a) and (b) are correct.

9.   Trading currencies on the black market is:

Hint   Black markets exist in diverse environments.

a.   severely punished by all governments.
b.   always more profitable.
c.   not very common.
d.   viewed differently by various governments around the globe. It may be condoned in one country and severely punished in another, as in the example of Brazil and Zimbabwe.

10. The exchange-rate arrangements of countries that are members of the IMF fall into three broad categories. They are:

Hint   The categories range from static to fluid.

   a.   pegged, flexible, and black market rates.
   b.   pegged, limited-flexibility, and fixed.
   c.   The IMF does not concern itself with exchange-rate arrangements.
   d.   pegged exchange rates, limited-flexibility arrangements, and more flexile arrangements.

INTERNET EXERCISES

Exercise 1.
IMF
http://www.imf.org
Familiarize yourself with this organization's history and various functions. Write a brief essay describing the IMF.

Exercise 2.
IMF
http://www.imf.org"> www.imf.org
Click on country Info. Then visit the Web sites of five countries include several from the G7 category such as Canada, the United States, and Germany and compare them to less-developed nations such as Bangladesh and Ethiopia, etc. How do the G7 countries differ from the less-developed countries in the profiles given? Compare each country's Central Bank and summaries of Disbursements and Repayments. How do your findings relate to Chapter 10? Discuss in a brief essay.

Exercise 3.
Federal Reserve Bank of New York
http://www.ny.frb.org/">www.ny.frb.org
Explore the history and several functional areas of the organization. Describe your findings and how they relate to Chapter 10 on exchange rates.

Exercise 4.
Thomas Cook
http://www.fx4business.com/qfgl.html
Visit this site on foreign exchange and click on the foreign Currency Forward category. How does this information relate to Chapters 9 and 10? Investigate several other categories of interest on this site and relate this to foreign exchange.

Exercise 5.
Association for the Monetary Union of Europe
http://amue.lf.net/welcome.html
Explore the links under Corporate Functions and relate your findings to Chapters 9 and 10. Discuss how the euro will impact foreign exchange forecasting in a brief essay.

CHAPTER 10 ANSWER KEY

True/False

1.   False   Yes, black markets for foreign exchange tend to continue in spite of government mandates.
     Difficulty: moderate
     Topic: Case: The Chinese Renminbi

2.   False   Yes, it is false to place the IMF creation before WWII. It was officially created on December 27, 1945, and began financial operations in March 1947.
     Difficulty: easy
     Topic: The International Monetary Fund

3.   True   Yes, The Bretton Wood Agreement became a benchmark by which each country's currency was valued against other currencies.
     Difficulty: moderate
     Topic: The International Monetary Fund

4.   True   Yes, the SDRs serve as the IMF's unit of account and supplement member's existing reserve assets such as official holdings of gold, foreign exchange.
     Difficulty: hard
     Topic: Special Drawing Rights (SDRs)

5.   False   Yes, it is not correct to state that the Jamaica Agreement of 1976 reinforced old exchange rate rules. Rather, the Agreement formalized the break from fixed exchange rates.
     Difficulty: moderate
     Topic: Evolution to Floating Exchange Rate

6.   True   Yes, as part of the IMF surveillance program, it monitors the economic policies of countries and exchange rate policies of countries.
     Difficulty: moderate
     Topic: Exchange-Rate Arrangements

7.   True   Yes, the New York Fed that represents the Federal Reserve System and the U.S. Treasury is responsible to oversee and counter disorderly conditions in foreign exchange markets.
     Difficulty: hard
     Topic: The Role of Central Banks

8.   False   Yes, countries vary in how they manage their reserves to earn a profit.
     Difficulty: hard
     Topic: The Role of Central Banks

9.   False   No, on the contrary, free-floating currencies tend to have a laissez-faire environment.
     Difficulty: easy
     Topic: The Determination of Exchange Rates

10. True   Yes that statement is correct.
     Difficulty: hard
     Topic: The Determination of Exchange Rates

Multiple Choice

1. b.   Yes, China has tried a number of strategies to monitor economic stability and gain access to foreign capital.
    Difficulty: moderate
    Topic: Case: The Chinese Renmimbi

2. c.   Yes, this describes the crawling pegs exchange rate.
    Difficulty: hard
    Topic: Exchange Rate Arrangements

3. a.   Yes, black markets for foreign exchange exist when demand exceeds supply because of exchange controls.
    Difficulty: moderate
    Topic: Black Markets

4. a.   Yes, the above methods are among the methods central banks may use to intervene in the currency market.
    Difficulty: hard
    Topic: The Role of Central Banks

5. d.   Yes, this is a good description of currencies that float freely.
    Difficulty: moderate
    Topic: The Determination of Exchange Rates

6. c.   Yes, this describes the PPP theory.
    Difficulty: hard
    Topic: Purchasing-Power Parity

7. b.   Yes, the fundamental approach uses trends in economic variables to predict future rates and the technical forecasting approach uses past trends in exchange rates themselves to spot future trends in rates.
    Difficulty: hard
    Topic: Forecasting Exchange-Rate Movements

8. b.   Yes, the exchange rates can impact marketing, production, and financial decision making of a company.
    Difficulty: moderate
    Topic: Business Implications of Exchange Rate Changes

9. d.   Yes, although black markets are illegal, they represent an ethical dilemma in the area of foreign exchange.
    Difficulty: moderate
    Topic: Ethical Dilemmas and Social Responsibilities

10. d.   Yes, these are the three broad categories, which the IMF then breaks down into several more specific categories.
    Difficulty: hard
    Topic: Summary

Chapter 11

Governmental Attitudes toward Foreign Direct Investment

CHAPTER OBJECTIVES

1. To examine the conflicting objectives of MNE stakeholders.

2. To discuss problems in evaluating MNE activities.

3. To evaluate the major economic impacts—balance of payments and growth—of MNEs on home and host countries.

4. To introduce the major criticisms about MNEs.

5. To provide an overview of the major political controversies surrounding MNE activities.

TRUE/FALSE

1. Chinese policy is to promote maximum self-sufficiency.

   Hint   China has political and cultural reasons somewhat separate from other countries.

2. China does not believe in special export zones (SEZs).

   Hint   China provides special incentives to encourage technology transfers and accumulation of foreign currencies.

3. The Chinese market potential is generally considered too marginal because of the Chinese low per capita income.

   Hint   China has the world's largest population.

4. The Chinese fear foreign cultural contamination.

   Hint   China monitors for behavioral standards.

5. Cross-national controversies are a thing of the past in light of the advanced global communications networks.

   Hint   Constituencies in any given country seek to fulfill their own, rather than global objectives.

6. FDIs always have a win-lose outcome.

   Hint   FDIs can have both a positive or negative impact on a host country.

7. Opponents to the FDI link and MNEs correctly identify and represent the evils of FDIs and MNEs.

   Hint   It is not certain what would have happened had MNEs not operated or not followed certain practices.

8. MNEs may affect a country's balance-of-payments either positively or negatively.

   Hint   Time and circumstances have different consequences.

9. A distinction about balance-of-payments is that gains are a zero sum.

    Hint   Zero-sum in this context contends that one country's trade or capital surplus is another's deficit.

10. The net capital flow is easy to calculate and always correct in the long run.

    Hint   Time lag creates problems with accurate assessments.

11. The effects of MNEs on employment growth can be win-win.

    Hint   MNEs can stimulate the economy.

12. Foreign investments in emerging economies tend to yield more growth than if they were located in developed countries.

    Hint   Emerging economies have great potential for growth.

13. Extraterritoriality exists when MNEs enforce home-country laws in a foreign country.

    Hint   Extraterritoriality was widely practiced under colonial rule.

14. The 1977 U.S. Foreign Corrupt Practices Act (FCPA) seeks to allow companies to engage in the host-country customs such as bribery.

    Hint   Bribery is illegal in the United States.

MULTIPLE CHOICE

1. Within the realm of Foreign Direct Investment, the Chinese Ministry of Foreign Trade and Economic Cooperation (MOFTEC) is one of the authorities to decide:

    Hint   China has not allowed investment to enter freely.

    a.   if the FDI should be confiscated.
    b.   the amount of the bribe an FDI should be charged.
    c.   if the investment is in the best interest of China.
    d.   None of the above is correct.

2. One important reason China may reward a foreign company an infrastructure project is that the company may:

    Hint   China is interested in modernizing.

    a.   transfer technology into China with the production process.
    b.   bring with it a source of cheap labor.
    c.   bring in more risqué pornographic materials that are unfamiliar to the Chinese.
    d.   implement extraterritoriality.

3. When considering production within China, a foreign company must first:

Hint   China has a command economy.

   a. learn to speak fluent Mandarin.
   b. find a sponsoring Chinese organization that will approve its application to establish a representative office.
   c. adapt to the Chinese technology.
   d. None of the above is correct.

4. The Chinese see two major benefits regarding FDI. These are:

Hint   Consider China's desire to modernize.

   a. increased interaction and cultural exchanges with foreigners and potential for export earnings.
   b. the potential for technology transfer and culture exchange.
   c. the transfer of technology and potential for increased exports from FDI investments.
   d. None of the above is correct.

5. The primary public concern about FDI is that MNEs involved in FDIs are:

Hint   Consider the need for sovereignty and national interest.

   a. going to make an adequate profit.
   b. going to conduct terrorist activities.
   c. going to hire home-country nationals.
   d. not properly concerned about host-country social issues because of their global outlook.

6. An MNE's actions within an FDI context may affect a country's:

Hint   MNEs have considerable power and influence.

   a. economic, social, and political objectives.
   b. major religious practices.
   c. economy only, all other facets are controllable.
   d. None of the above is correct.

7. Some beneficial contributions MNEs make in the area of human resources are:

Hint   MNEs need a skilled labor force.

   a. the open invitation for employees to form labor unions.
   b. bringing a skilled labor force from other world sites.
   c. employee training for the local population in the area of needed production and managerial skills.
   d. training local managers and transferring them to the MNE's home country.

8. The effects of MNEs on growth and employment are:

Hint   Circumstances determine outcomes.

   a. the home country always loses and the host country gains.
   b. the economic benefits to a host country do not justify the exploitation of its labor force.
   c. not necessarily a zero-sum game.
   d. devastating to the home country.

9. Some of the resources a foreign investor may have access to that local companies cannot easily acquire include:

   Hint Consider the broad access to resources MNEs have around the globe.

   a. capital and domestic markets.
   b. capital, management skills, and external markets.
   c. domestic capital and external markets.
   d. local companies have the same advantage as MNEs.

10. Although extraterritoriality may result from legal differences between any two countries, _____ has been most often criticized for attempting to control their companies abroad.

    Hint Consider the country with the most powerful and largest number of MNEs.

    a. Britain
    b. Sweden
    c. Extraterritoriality no longer exists.
    d. the United States

11. The Berlin-based organization Transparency International's mission is to:

    Hint This organization is concerned with fair dealings.

    a. market plastic materials.
    b. assist citizens to enhance bribery deals.
    c. assist citizens in setting up national chapters to try to fight local bribery.
    d. both (a) and (c) are correct.

12. According to the Transparency International opinion survey conducted, which ranked the perception of executives regarding 19 leading exporting country's bribery activities, the four countries rated highest and most likely to engage in bribery were:

    Hint The poll was conducted by Gallop International and collected opinions from bankers, accountants, lawyers, and the chamber of commerce.

    a. Sweden, China, Canada, and South Korea.
    b. China, South Korea, Taiwan, and Italy.
    c. Japan, France, Singapore, and the United States.
    d. Spain, Belgium, Britain, and Germany.

13. Governments regulate FDI to improve their balance-of-payments positions by:

    Hint Consider what host governments will see as beneficial to their constituents.

    a. encouraging local borrowing by foreign investors.
    b. restricting capital flows, requiring partial local ownership of FDI, limiting local borrowing by foreign investors, and stipulating that a part of capital inflows must be in the form of loans rather than equity.
    c. Governments do not regulate FDIs.
    d. None of the above is correct.

14. South Africa initiated a plan in 1999 to attract FDI by:

   Hint   Consider internal development and spin-offs.

   a.   South Africa does not encourage FDI.
   b.   encouraging migration of labor for the home countries of the MNEs.
   c.   enforcing apartheid laws.
   d.   offering $5 billion in defense contracts to foreign companies.

15. Some of the concerns from foreign companies who are considering FDI are:

   Hint   Consider risk management and opportunities.

   a.   the costs of complying with government affirmative action programs, lack of skilled labor, and government officials' requests for bribery.
   b.   South Africa's policy of apartheid.
   c.   lack of developed infrastructure.
   d.   low domestic market due to a small population.

INTERNET EXERCISES

Exercise 1.
Transparency International
http://www.transparency.de/
Learn about Transparency International's overall mission and history. Write a brief essay on the role this organization plays in international trade.

Exercise 2.
National Business Initiative (NBI)
http://www.nbi.org.za
Click on the government, business, issues, and labor links. Reflect on how this organization is promoting South Africa and relate it to the case in the text. Describe your findings in a brief essay.

Exercise 3.
Office of the Chief Counsel for International Commerce
http://www.ita.doc.gov/legal
Access the materials on transparency and antibribery initiative links. Describe your findings in a sucking overview.

Exercise 4.
Office of the Chief Counsel for International Commerce
http://www.ita.doc.gov/legal
Click on Foreign Corrupt Practices Act: An Overview. Then click and read the information on several other links to the Foreign Corrupt Practices Act. Describe the Foreign Corrupt Practices Act and current concerns on bribery. Relate this to the section on bribery in the text.

Exercise 5.
African National Congress
http://www.anc.org.za/sanet.html
Go to the South African Internet Resources site and take the role of a decision maker on FDIs for an MNE. Inform yourself on the potential for FDI by visiting appropriate links. Then write a proposal to top management on the opportunities of considering an FDI in South Africa.

CHAPTER 11 ANSWER KEY

True/False

1. **True** Yes, China has long practiced a form of isolationism and has encouraged self-sufficiency.
   Difficulty: moderate
   Topic: Case: Foreign Direct Investment in China

2. **False** Yes, although China encourages self-sufficiency, it also promotes certain FDIs.
   Difficulty: moderate
   Topic: Case: Foreign Direct Investment in China

3. **False** Yes, The Chinese market size overrides low per capita income considerations for companies such as GM.
   Difficulty: hard
   Topic: Case: Foreign Direct Investment in China

4. **True** Yes, China is concerned about improper ethical and moral standards that conflict with national ideology.
   Difficulty: moderate
   Topic: Case: Foreign Direct Investment in China

5. **False** Yes, it is incorrect to assume that cross-national controversies no longer exist in light of new and powerful lobbying groups such as environmentalists and human rights advocates.
   Difficulty: moderate
   Topic: Evaluating the Impact of FDI

6. **False** On the contrary, careful negotiations on terms tend to make the FDI and host-country outcomes win-win.
   Difficulty: hard
   Topic: Trade-offs among Objectives

7. **False** The issue of FDI and related costs and benefits are not easily resolved because both proponents and opponents tend to portray only their side of the issue.
   Difficulty: moderate
   Topic: Cause-Effect Relationships

8. **True** Yes, the balance-of-payments effect on a country because of FDI and MNE activity must be analyzed within the context of time, activities, and other contingencies.
   Difficulty: hard
   Topic: Economic Impact of the MNE

9. **True** Yes, in the case of balance-of-payments the loss of one country is the gain of another.
   Difficulty: hard
   Topic: Economic Impact of the MNE

10. **False** Capital flow calculations do not lend themselves to long-run scenarios.
    Difficulty: hard
    Topic: Economic Impact of the MNE

11. **True** Yes, rather than being a predictable a zero-sum game, MNEs can stimulate employment growth in their home countries as well as abroad.
    Difficulty: hard
    Topic: Growth and Employment Effects

12. True   Yes, developed countries do not have equal growth potential as developing countries.
Difficulty: easy
Topic: Growth and Employment Effects

13. True   Yes, the concept of extraterritoriality occurs when MNEs enforce laws from their home government.
Difficulty: moderate
Topic: Extraterritoriality

14. False   The FCPA is an attempt to curtail bribery rather than encourage it.
Difficulty: easy
Topic: Bribery

Multiple Choice

1. c.   Yes, the MOFTEC along with other provincial-level authorities has jurisdiction over certain types of investments.
Difficulty: easy
Topic: Case: Foreign Direct Investment in China

2. a.   Yes, China considers FDIs favorably if they also transfer desirable technology into China.
Difficulty: easy
Topic: Case: Foreign Direct Investment in China

3. b.   Yes, FDIs need to be sponsored, which is another form of approval, in order to establish itself in China.
Difficulty: moderate
Topic: Case: Foreign Direct Investment in China

4. c.   Yes, the Chinese consider the two most important FDI benefits to result in the transfer of technology and export earnings in foreign exchange.
Difficulty: easy
Topic: Case: Foreign Direct Investment in China

5. d.   Yes, critiques worry about an MNE's intent regarding host-country national and social issues.
Difficulty: moderate
Topic: Introduction

6. a.   Yes, MNEs can have a significant overall impact on a host country.
Difficulty: moderate
Topic: Evaluating the Impact of FDI

7. c.   Yes, this example indicates some of the benefits a MNE can bring to the host country.
Difficulty: moderate
Topic: Potential Contributions of MNEs

8. c.   Yes, it is important to remember that gains and losses are not always consistent when considering capital movements. Current strategies tend to position strategies for win-win outcomes for stakeholders on both sides.
Difficulty: hard
Topic: Growth and Employment Effects

9. b.   Yes, MNEs tend to have easier access to capital, have highly skilled managerial talents, and have extensive external markets.
Difficulty: easy
Topic: Host-Country Losses

10. d.   Yes, the United States has been criticized the most for attempting to control U.S. companies abroad.
     Difficulty: moderate
     Topic: Extraterritoriality

11. c.   Yes, this organization's mission is to fight bribery worldwide.
     Difficulty: moderate
     Topic: Bribery

12. b.   Yes, these countries were ranked highest by the Transparency International sponsored study on bribery.
     Difficulty: easy
     Topic: Likelihood of Paying Bribes Abroad by Nationality of Companies, Figure 11.4

13. b.   Yes, the above response correctly identifies the most significant tools governments use to regulate FDIs.
     Difficulty: moderate
     Topic: Summary

14. d.   Yes, the conditions to the defense contracts are that the companies will have to provide state-of-the art weapons and equipment and must develop new investments in South Africa.
     Difficulty: moderate
     Topic: Case: FDI in South Africa

15. a.   Yes, these concerns are prominent for companies considering FDI in South Africa.
     Difficulty: moderate
     Topic: Case: FDI in South Africa

Chapter 12

International Business Negotiations and Diplomacy

CHAPTER OBJECTIVES

1.   To show the common and conflicting interests between countries and MNEs.

2.   To illustrate negotiations between business and government in an international context.

3.   To trace the changing roles of home-country governments in settling an MNE's disputes with host governments.

4.   To clarify the role of companies' public affairs and political behavior in international business.

5.   To explain the position of companies and governments in the uneven global enforcement of intellectual property rights.

TRUE/FALSE

1.   U.S. policy toward U.S. oil companies historically has fostered safeguarding sufficient and cheap oil supplies for U.S. needs.

      Hint   The United States is an industrialized country that depends on ready oil supplies.

2.   Standard Oil of California and Exxon were the first two U.S. oil companies to participate in Saudi Arabian oil production.

      Hint   Consider name changes for oil companies.

3.   When King Ibn Saud demanded substantial revenue increases from Aramco; the U.S. government practiced laissez-faire politics.

      Hint   The U.S. government supports the safeguarding of its oil supply.

4.   After the Saudi government took complete ownership of Aramco, it began to replace foreign technicians and reserved the top management position for foreign executives.

      Hint   The Saudi government wanted to insure control of Aramco.

5.   Governments have regulations affecting international business.

      Hint   Governments seek to protect their constituents.

6.   The Bargain School Theory holds that the negotiated terms for a foreign investor's operations depend on how much the investor and host country need each other's assets.

      Hint   Good bargaining tries to have a win-win situation.

7.   Agriculture and extractive industries have a bad image in FDI.

      Hint   Consider the dominant activities in the colonial period.

8. The home country usually takes a neutral position when companies and foreign governments bargain for FDI terms.

   Hint   Home and host countries both have stakes in the bargaining process.

9. Most countries offer investment incentives to attract MNEs.

   Hint   Host-country governments consider the gains in FDIs.

10. A company's best bargaining position exists before it makes an investment in a foreign country.

   Hint   Consider the effect on bargaining once assets have been moved.

11. Cultural factors do not impact business negotiations.

   Hint   Sublet issues may become important issues.

12. Government and business negotiators tend to start with mutual trust regardless of past differences or professional status.

   Hint   Perceptions affect negotiations.

13. Companies considering FDI are concerned that foreign countries will appropriate their assets without receiving adequate compensation for them.

   Hint   Consider the case of Cuba.

14. All countries are members of the various conventions to protect Intellectual Property Rights (IPRs).

   Hint   IPRs are a source of global concern.

15. Coca-Cola and IBM have had an easy operating experience in India.

   Hint   Strict operating restrictions in India have led to company adjustments.

MULTIPLE CHOICE

1. The companies known as the Seven Sisters consisted of:

   Hint   The Seven Sisters consisted of a consortium of oil companies.

   a.   Socal, Texaco, Aramco, Mobil Gulf, Shell, and BP.
   b.   various female religious sects.
   c.   Exxon, Mobil, Socal, Texaco, Gulf, Shell, and BP.
   d.   The Seven Sisters is not a concept of international business.

2. The Caracas meeting in the 1960s that led to the formation of the Organization of Petroleum Exporting Countries (OPEC) consisted of representatives from five oil-producing countries. These countries were:

    Hint   The majority of the countries came from the Middle East.

    a. Egypt, Iran, Iraq, Mexico, and Kuwait.
    b. Saudi Arabia, Iran, Iraq, Venezuela, and Libya.
    c. The Caracas meeting did not have five countries represented and it did not lead to the formation of OPEC.
    d. Iran, Iraq, Kuwait, Saudi Arabia, and Venezuela.

3. Generally, companies prefer to establish investments in highly developed countries because:

    Hint   Consider risk management and opportunities.

    a. companies do not favor investing in developed countries.
    b. those countries have a low crime rate and cheap labor.
    c. they offer large markets and political stability.
    d. Both (b) and (c) are correct.

4. To counter too high a dependence on foreign companies, countries have:

    Hint   Consider internal strength to counter external threats.

    a. reduced tariffs.
    b. offered incentives to FDIs.
    c. invested abroad.
    d. encouraged their domestic industries to consolidate to counter foreign companies' strengths.

5. Negotiations are a means by which a company may:

    Hint   Consider the various interests of companies.

    a. use bribery to secure a contract.
    b. terminate operations in a foreign country.
    c. initiate, carry on, or terminate operations.
    d. None of the above is correct.

6. Like domestic negotiations, international negotiations tend to:

    Hint   Consider the options within the negotiation window.

    a. disregard macroeconomic conditions.
    b. have no zones of acceptance.
    c. use recent events as reference points.
    d. be strictly business and objective and do not take qualitative factors such as culture into consideration.

7. Cultural and behavioral characteristics affect international negotiations in that:

    Hint   Culture is the foundation of perception.

    a. Culture does not affect negotiations, only language does.
    b. there may be problems when socializing together.
    c. there may be irrevocable misunderstandings due to cultural differences.
    d. None of the above is correct.

8. When English is used as the negotiating language and only one party is a native to the language the:

Hint   Interpreters may take liberties with the language.

   a.   English-speaking person is at a disadvantage.
   b.   English-speaking person is at a distinct advantage.
   c.   English is only used as the negotiating language if both parties are familiar with English.
   d.   negotiations tend to run more smoothly.

9. Bilateral treaties tend to provide home country:

Hint   Treaties are agreements between governments.

   a.   hands-off policies because of the risk involved.
   b.   insurance to investors to cover losses.
   c.   Bilateral treaties are no longer made.
   d.   Both (a) and (c) are correct.

10. The key area of business-government and government-to-government conflicts in international business recently have been related to:

Hint   Knowledge-based assets are in high demand.

   a.   education programs related to exchange students.
   b.   intellectual property rights (IPRs).
   c.   solving the problem of world poverty.
   d.   countering the strict IPR legislation in developing countries.

11. Piracy of IPRs:

Hint   Consider the consequences of stolen property.

   a.   may have mixed results for consumers.
   b.   benefits the property owner.
   c.   is condoned by developed countries.
   d.   is most vigorously fought in less-developed countries.

12. The first major attempt to achieve cross-national cooperation in the protection of patents, trademarks, and other property rights was the _____.

Hint   IPRs have long been a concern of industrialized countries.

   a.   Bretton Woods Conference in 1944
   b.   Treaty of Rome in 1957
   c.   WTO conference in Seattle in 1999
   d.   Paris Convention in 1883

13. Shortly after World War II, some of the organizations that were created to regulate international companies were:

Hint   The organizations emphasized global issues.

   a.   the League of Nations and the WTO.
   b.   the International Trade Organization (ITO), the United Nations Economic and Social Council (ECOSCO), and the Organization for Economic Cooperation and Development (OECD).
   c.   NAFTA and ASEAN.
   d.   No attempt has been made to regulate international companies.

14. The present welcoming of FDI could easily reverse if governments feel that:

Hint   Governments monitor for their constituents.

   a.   international human rights issues are not addressed.
   b.   their own citizens are not receiving a just share of global economic benefits.
   c.   Governments will always be in favor of FDI.
   d.   It is unlikely that the present welcoming of FDI would be reversed.

15. Some governments have used _____ to ensure that the terms agreed on between their investors and host countries would be carried out.

Hint   Consider past actions by governments that are seen as disreputable today.

   a.   Governments do not become involved to ensure that the terms their companies make in a host country are carried out.
   b.   military intervention and coercion
   c.   Foreign companies may not expect to have terms honored in a foreign country because of the differences in legal systems.
   d.   Both (b) and (c) are correct.

INTERNET EXERCISES

Exercise 1.
World Intellectual Property Organization
http://www.wipo.org
Explore the site. Get a sense of this organization's mission. Click on at least five links to get a sense of this organization and how it relates to trade. Then write a descriptive report to explain the WIPO and how it relates to international trade.

Exercise 2.
Saudi Aramco
http://www.aramco.com
Click on "about us" and "operations" links. How does the present Aramco Company compare to the former Seven Sisters operation described in the text? Relate this information to the discussions in chapter 12.

Exercise 3.
WTO
http://www.wto.org
Click on the trade topics and relate them to the discussions in Chapter 12 in a succinct essay.

Essay 4.
OECD
http://www.oecd.org
Become familiar with this organization's mission. Relate this organization's mission to the topics in Chapter 12.

Exercise 5.
Enron
http://www.ect.enron.com
Discuss this company's global outreach strategies as evident from this Web site. Relate this to this companies experience as described in Chapter 12 in a brief descriptive essay.

CHAPTER 12 ANSWER KEY

True/False

1. **True**   Yes, the U.S. position on oil has been strategic and worldwide to ensure a continuous oil supply.
    Difficulty: easy
    Topic: Case: Saudi Aramco.

2. **False**   No, Socal—Standard Oil of California and Exxon are the same company. Texaco was the other company, which initiated oil production in Saudi Arabia.
    Difficulty: moderate
    Topic: Case: Saudi Aramco

3. **True**   No, the U.S. government became involved in the negotiation process with Saudi Arabia's king Ibn Saud.
    Difficulty: moderate
    Topic: Case: Saudi Aramco

4. **False**   Yes, it is not correct to assume that the Saudi government would relinquish control to foreigners once it took possession of Aramco. Instead, it began to replace foreign management with Saudi management until Saudis held all top positions.
    Difficulty: easy
    Topic: Case: Saudi Aramco

5. **True**   Yes, governments monitor international business to insure their interests are fairly represented.
    Difficulty: easy
    Topic: Governmental versus Company Strength in Negotiations

6. **True**   Yes, this statement is true and considers that one-sided negotiations do not lead to good bargaining.
    Difficulty: moderate
    Topic: Bargain View

7. **True**   Yes, because of historical foreign domination in agriculture and extraction and the belief that land and subsoil are public resources these industries unwelcome as FDIs.
    Difficulty: hard
    Topic: Company Bargaining Strength

8. **False**   Yes, it is wrong to assume that a home-country government would be neutral in the terms a home company receives with a foreign government because economic considerations will also impact the home country.
    Difficulty: hard
    Topic: Home-Country Needs

9. **True**   Yes, host governments offer direct incentives such as tax holidays, R&D grants, loan guarantees, and subsidized energy to entice foreign investors.
    Difficulty: moderate
    Topic: Range of Provisions

10. **True**   Yes, generally speaking, a company is in a better position to bargain for attractive terms before it commits to an FDI.
    Difficulty: easy
    Topic: Renegotiations

11. False   Yes, it is false to state that culture is not important to negotiations. Cultural factors must be understood, otherwise there may be misunderstandings or negotiation may fail.
    Difficulty: moderate
    Topic: Cultural Factors

12. False   On the contrary, negotiator may bring with them assumptions that interfere with establishing a base of trust.
    Difficulty: moderate
    Topic: Professional Conflict

13. True   Yes, companies consider the risks to assets when investing them in another country.
    Difficulty: moderate
    Topic: Home-Country Involvement in Asset Protection

14. False   IPRs are not recognized by all countries, and piracy and counterfeiting is rampant around the globe.
    Difficulty: hard
    Topic: Piracy

15. False   Yes, it is false to assert that the above companies found operating in India to be easy. Instead, both Coca-Cola and IBM left India at about the same time because of Indian government regulations.
    Difficulty: easy
    Topic: Case: PepsiCo in India

Multiple Choice

1. c.   Yes, the first four companies became Aramco.
   Difficulty: easy
   Topic: Case: Saudi Aramco

2. d.   Yes, the above five countries sent representatives to the meeting in Caracas, which ultimately led to the formation of OPEC.
   Difficulty: easy
   Topic: Case: Saudi Aramco

3. c.   Yes, this tends to be the reason why developed countries are preferred for investments.
   Difficulty: moderate
   Topic: Country Bargaining Strength

4. d.   Yes, one example is the European consortium that built the Airbus to counter the Boeing aircraft industry.
   Difficulty: easy
   Topic: Joint Company Activities

5. c.   Yes, negotiators have a broad range of options to use in the bargaining process.
   Difficulty: easy
   Topic: Negotiations in International Business

6. c.   Yes, both negotiating parties will consider situational factors within their negations.
   Difficulty: moderate
   Topic: Bargaining Process

7. c.   Yes, cultural differences may create serious misunderstandings.
   Difficulty: hard
   Topic: Behavioral Characteristics Affecting Negotiations

8.　a.　　　　Yes, interpreters may misinterpret the original and the English-speaking person will not know this.
　　　Difficulty: moderate
　　　Topic:　　Behavioral Characteristics Affecting Negotiations

9.　b.　　　　Yes, treaties tend to include insurance to cover losses such as: losses from expropriation, political violence, governmental contract cancellation, and currency related losses.
　　　Difficulty: hard
　　　Topic:　　The Use of Bilateral Agreements

10.　b.　　　Yes, IPRs are the cause of much disagreement and conflict in international business today.
　　　Difficulty: hard
　　　Topic:　　Mutual Agreements: IPRs

11.　a.　　　Yes, although piracy is a crime, consumers may benefit in the short run by being able to purchase cheaper, "imitation" goods.
　　　Difficulty: hard
　　　Topic:　　Piracy

12.　d.　　　Yes, this initiated cross-national cooperation for the protection of patents, trademarks, and other property rights.
　　　Difficulty: moderate
　　　Topic:　　Patents.

13.　b.　　　Yes, these are some of the organizations that attempted to regulate international companies soon after WWII. The ITO never became operable however.
　　　Difficulty: hard
　　　Topic:　　Collective Actions to Deal with International Companies

14.　b.　　　Yes, governments tend to be concerned about fairness for their citizens when negotiating for FDI.
　　　Difficulty: hard
　　　Topic:　　Looking to the Future

15.　b.　　　Yes, aggressive retaliation has been used to ensure compliance for a home-company's agreed-upon terms.
　　　Difficulty: hard
　　　Topic:　　Summary

Chapter 13

Country Evaluation and Selection

CHAPTER OBJECTIVES

1. To discuss company strategies for sequencing the penetration of countries and committing resources.

2. To explain how clues from the environmental climate can help managers limit geographic alternatives.

3. To examine the major variables a company should consider when deciding whether and where to expand abroad.

4. To overview methods and problems of collecting and comparing information internationally.

5. To describe some simplifying tools for determining a global geographic strategy.

6. To introduce how managers make final investment, reinvestment, and divestment decisions.

TRUE/FALSE

1. Blockbuster targeted high-income industrialized countries in the beginning.

    Hint   Blockbuster customers use relatively expensive equipment.

2. Committing human, technical, and financial resources to one locale may mean foregoing projects in other areas.

    Hint   Companies seldom have enough resources to take advantage of all opportunities.

3. A company's country selection process does not need careful analysis because everyone in the world needs products.

    Hint   Companies should look to those countries with economic, political, cultural, and geographic conditions that mesh with its strengths.

4. Decisions on market and production locations tend to be very complex.

    Hint   Market and production locations may be highly interdependent.

5. Determining geographic strategies are among the easiest decisions, as geography stays the same.

    Hint   Country conditions change.

6. Scanning techniques to compare potential county sites are too superficial to be useful.

    Hint   Scanning is like weeding out.

7. The environmental climate in a host country is a term used to assess weather conditions in targeted locations.

    Hint   Environmental climate considers conditions in a host country that could significantly affect the success or failure of a foreign business venture.

8. Sales potential is probably the most important variable managers use in determining where and whether to make an investment.

Hint   Markets are the main reason why companies go international.

9. The triad market is targeted by most MNEs.

Hint   The triad consists of North America, Japan, and Western Europe.

10. Lead country strategy tests products in a small market.

Hint   Consider the example of Optim shampoo in Hong Kong.

11. Companies always choose locations for the least-cost production.

Hint   Consider the example of BMW's choice to forego a Mexican plant.

12. Because red tape is not measurable, companies tend to minimize it.

Hint   Red tape increases operating costs.

13. Liquidity Preference Theory can be applied to domestic as well as international expansion decisions.

Hint   Liquidity Preference Theory is the theory that states that investors want some of their holdings to be in highly liquid assets.

14. Research on some countries may be too expensive to undertake.

Hint   Data is not always consistent or accurate.

15. New investment decisions and reinvestment decisions are treated the same.

Hint   Goals may be different for new investments and old ones.

MULTIPLE CHOICE

1. Blockbuster initiated its major foreign expansion by targeting:

Hint   Blockbuster customers use expensive equipment.

   a.   developing countries.
   b.   the EU.
   c.   the industrial countries of Canada, Europe, and Japan.
   d.   South America.

2. A company's geographic strategy should be flexible enough to:

Hint   Country conditions change.

   a.   allow for quick opening or downsizing of plants to minimize nationalization.
   b.   respond to new opportunities and withdraw from less lucrative ones.
   c.   bring employees from the home office to the host country quickly.
   d.   Companies do not consider flexibility in country selection.

3. In assessing international location expansion decisions, the environmental climate refers to:

Hint   Environments are external.

a. external conditions in a host country that could significantly affect the success or failure of a foreign company.
b. regulations concerning pollution and industrial waste.
c. home-country laws.
d. Both (a) and (c) are correct.

4. Sales potential is probably the most important variable in determining location and investment decisions providing that:

Hint   Consider the underlying motive for sales.

a. sales will generate a profit.
b. supply exceeds demand.
c. customers are friendly.
d. governments use a form of protectionism.

5. At the early stages of international expansion, managers feel more comfortable:

Hint   The familiar is comfortable.

a. in developing countries, which depend on the company.
b. with an interpreter and a highly skilled staff of experts from the host country.
c. Managers never feel comfortable with international expansion.
d. doing business in their own language and in a familiar legal system.

6. Blockbuster failed in Germany because:

Hint   Blockbuster could not duplicate the successful formula it practiced elsewhere.

a. Germans do not watch videos.
b. Germans wanted a larger selection of family movies, which Blockbuster did not carry.
c. German stores are regulated by operating hours that conflicted with the Blockbuster peak operating period.
d. Blockbuster's venture in Germany was a big success.

7. Figures on national income and per capita income are difficult to compare because:

Hint   Countries differ in production methods and measurements for personal production.

a. exchange rates fluctuate.
b. various production activities may not be recorded.
c. national and per capita incomes are easy to compare.
d. None of the above is correct.

8. Reasons for inaccuracies in government published data include:

    Hint   Resources and motives can influence data compilation.

    a.   All government reports are factual.
    b.   limited resources, incompetent officials, and falsification of records to present a more favorable picture of the country.
    c.   the fact that old journals are being used.
    d.   poor editing and improper use of grammar.

9. Companies may gain advantages in locating where competitors are because:

    Hint   A follower may get a "free ride."

    a.   companies do not have an advantage where there are competitors.
    b.   competitors will be easily eliminated.
    c.   customers are disloyal and will switch easily.
    d.   suppliers, skilled personnel, and relevant information for that industry are readily available.

10. The three approaches managers use to predict political risks are:

    Hint   Consider the patterns within a conceptual overview.

    a.   Political risks are not analyzed by companies; this is a function of the home government.
    b.   studying past patterns, seeking information from experts, and analyzing present social, political, and economic conditions in the targeted country.
    c.   investing and then monitoring for political changes, using extraterritoriality as a tool and establishing an information database.
    d.   Companies do not consider countries with political risks.

11. A major difficulty in using data from country research is:

    Hint   Countries use different reporting criteria.

    a.   the language is not English.
    b.   comparability problems.
    c.   it is secret information.
    d.   it is very costly to obtain.

12. Two popular matrices managers use when comparing countries are:

    Hint   Managers consider costs and benefits when making assessments.

    a.   the risk matrix and the opportunity matrix.
    b.   Managers do not use this model; rather they use the intuitive approach.
    c.   the opportunity-risk and country attractiveness-company strength matrices.
    d.   None of the above is correct.

13.   When companies reduce commitments in a country because of anticipated poor performance, this process is known as:

Hint   Consider the situation in that it would limit the use of new resource investments.

a.   passive investments.
b.   closure.
c.   harvesting.
d.   reinvesting.

14.   The strategy describing a company's rapid moves into many foreign markets is called:

Hint   Consider that the moves will be varied.

a.   concentration strategy.
b.   diversification strategy.
c.   divestment strategy.
d.   concentrated divestment strategy.

15.   Once a feasibility study is complete, most companies:

Hint   Consider the go-no-go process.

a.   rank investment alternatives.
b.   set some minimum-threshold criteria and either reject or accept a foreign-based project on those criteria.
c.   Feasibility is never so complete that companies may act on it.
d.   None of the responses are correct.

INTERNET EXERCISES

Exercise 1.
Blockbuster
http://www.blockbuster.com
Learn about the company, the location of its stores, and franchising opportunities. Consider how this company has changed in relation to the company overview in the text case. Discuss how this relates to company strategy and the concepts in Chapter 13 in a succinct essay.

Exercise 2.
Colgate-Palmolive
http://www.colgate.com
Conduct a "tour of Colgate." Then learn about its products and investor relations strategy. How does Colgate-Palmolive position itself to the global market? Discuss.

Exercise 3.
Summit Analytical Associates
http://www.s2a.com/emcrisis.html
Explore the services this organization provides and how this relates to risk assessments discussed in Chapter 13. Click on the Risk Analysis link and write a brief overview of your findings and how these relate to the section on Risk in Chapter 13.

Exercise 4.
OECD
http://www.oecd.org
Explore various links to get an overview of this organization. Then focus on the statistics link and open it to "main economic indicators" and then the Composite Leading Indicators (CLI) section. Consider the resources within this rich environment and describe the resources by taking the position of a research analyst to show the value of this OECD site for companies considering FDI.

Exercise 5.
Shell Oil
http://www.shell.com/royal-en and http://www.cnn.com/WORLD/9703/24/nigeria.shell/
Compare your findings to the information in the Shell in Nigeria case. What additional information is available on this site to show the Nigeria/Shell relationship? In your opinion, is the risk to Royal Dutch Shell's presence in Nigeria greater now or less than the time when the case in the test was written? Explain.

CHAPTER 13 ANSWER KEY

True/False

1. **True**   Yes, industrialized countries tend to also have high per capita incomes that allow VCR purchases.
    Difficulty: easy
    Topic: Case: Blockbuster Video

2. **True**   Yes, companies must choose carefully to pick the best location, and this requires that some locations not be chosen.
    Difficulty: easy
    Topic: Introduction

3. **False**   Yes, it is not correct to assume that a company's country selection process should be undertaken lightly.
    Difficulty: easy
    Topic: Introduction

4. **True**   Yes, a company may have excess production capacity already in one location and this may influence its ability to serve markets in other countries.
    Difficulty: moderate
    Topic: Choosing Marketing and Production Sites, and Geographic Strategy

5. **False**   Yes, it is not a simple task to determine geographic strategies because the counties located in specific regions may undergo changes that affect strategic decisions.
    Difficulty: moderate
    Topic: Choosing Marketing and Production Sites, and Geographic Strategy

6. **False**   Yes, scanning is indeed a useful technique because it is based on broad variables that indicate opportunities and risks.
    Difficulty: moderate
    Topic: Scan for Alternative Locations

7. **False**   No, one should not simplify the phrase "environmental climate" to assume it means weather conditions when used in international business.
    Difficulty: easy
    Topic: Choose and Weight Variables

8. **True**   Yes, sales potential is critical (assuming that sales will also produce profit).
    Difficulty: moderate
    Topic: Market size

9. **True**   Yes, the triad market accounts for about half of the world's total consumption and is a lucrative market.
    Difficulty: hard
    Topic: Market Size

10. **True**   Yes, lead country strategies are strategies that focus on introducing a product in one country to test for larger market penetration in the region.
    Difficulty: moderate
    Topic: Ease and Compatibility of Operations

11. **False**   Yes, although production costs are important, companies also consider the place of production when preserving a high-quality image.
    Difficulty: moderate
    Topic: Costs and Resource Availability

12. **False** Yes, it is false to state that companies do not consider red tape an important consideration in location decisions.

Difficulty: moderate

Topic: Red Tape

13. **True** Yes, this theory holds true in the international business environment as well as in the home country.

Difficulty: hard

Topic: Monetary Risk

14. **True** Yes, data discrepancies can create uncertainties, and research may become too expensive to undertake in such cases.

Difficulty: moderate

Topic: Problems with Research Results and Data

15. **False** No, the above statement does not consider the difference between continuity and innovation.

Difficulty: moderate

Topic: Summary

Multiple Choice

1. c. Yes, these locations are among the world's highest-income countries and this was a logical move because video rentals also require ownership of VCRs that are relatively expensive.

Difficulty: easy

Topic: Case: Blockbuster Video

2. b. Yes, although there is little agreement on a comprehensive technique for choosing the best location, companies consider flexibility to take advantage of opportunities.

Difficulty: moderate

Topic: Choosing Marketing and Production Sites, and Geographic Strategy

3. a. Yes, this describes environmental climate with regard to international business.

Difficulty: moderate

Topic: Choose and Weigh Variables

4. a. Yes, sales are considered the most important variable assuming that the sale will result in a profit.

Difficulty: moderate

Topic: Market Size

5. d. Yes, a familiar environment tends to ease the pressure of operating in a different country, and it is for this reason that many U.S. managers prefer to operate in Canada or the U.K.

Difficulty: moderate

Topic: Ease and Compatibility of Operations

6. c. Yes, German law prevents evening, Sunday, and holiday operating hours, and these are the peak hours for video rentals.

Difficulty: hard

Topic: Case: Blockbuster Video

7. b. Yes, for instance, in many cases personal production of food and clothing is generally not counted as personal income.

Difficulty: hard

Topic: Problems with Research Results and Data

8. b.   Yes, these are some of the reasons why some government records are not believable.
    Difficulty: moderate
    Topic: Reasons for Inaccuracies

9. d.   Yes, resources are more readily available where competitors already have established a base, and this creates an advantage for companies who follow.
    Difficulty: hard
    Topic: Competitive Risk

10. b.   Yes, considering the past, studying the present, and seeking expert help is the method used by most managers to assess political risks.
    Difficulty: moderated
    Topic: Political Risk

11. b.   Yes, comparability is difficult because countries use different measuring systems, and these include demographic data, income analysis, and accounting systems.
    Difficulty: hard
    Topic: Comparability Problems

12. c.   The two popular matrices managers use when comparing countries are: the opportunity-risk and country attractiveness-company strength matrices.
    Difficulty: moderate
    Topic: Matrices

13. c.   Yes, harvesting or divesting is the term used to describe a company's strategy to reduce commitment if poor performance results as anticipated.
    Difficulty: hard
    Topic: Allocating Among Locations

14. b.   Yes, a diversification strategy is a company's effort to move and commit to many different foreign markets.
    Difficulty: hard
    Topic: Diversification versus Concentration

15. b.   Yes, this type of decision results because multiple feasibility studies seldom are finished simultaneously, and there may be pressures to act quickly.
    Difficulty: hard
    Topic: Summary

Chapter 14

Collaborative Strategies

CHAPTER OBJECTIVES

1. To explain the major motives that guide managers when choosing a collaborative arrangement for international business.

2. To define the major types of collaborative arrangements.

3. To describe what companies should consider when entering into arrangements with other companies.

4. To discuss what makes collaborative arrangements succeed or fail.

5. To discuss how companies can manage diverse collaborative arrangements.

TRUE/FALSE

1. Foreign companies seek out partnerships with Grupo Industrial Alfa because it knows how to deal with the Mexican bureaucracy.

   Hint   Alfa is an old Mexican company.

2. Foreign trademarks are frequently used by Mexican companies that partner with the foreign trademark holder.

   Hint   Consumers prefer a well-known trademark.

3. Once a company chooses an operating mode in a foreign location, it can no longer produce in its home country.

   Hint   Companies have many production site choices.

4. When collaboration is of strategic importance to one or more of the companies, it is known as a strategic alliance.

   Hint   Strategic goals may drive the motivation in a partnership.

5. McDonald's only franchises its operations in the United States and owns the foreign operations completely.

   Hint   McDonalds uses similar domestic and foreign strategies in its franchising operations.

6. A company that has excess production or sales capacity has only one option, which is to reduce production.

   Hint   Excess production can be channeled to needed areas.

7. Large, diversified companies prefer to keep their product line diverse rather than focusing on only a few.

   Hint   Companies tend to focus on core competencies.

8. Collusion is condoned in many countries.

   Hint   Consortiums tend towards collusion.

9. Companies may seek collaboration with local companies to overcome cultural barriers.

   Hint A foreign location has many barriers to overcome.

10. Collaborative agreements with local companies can help prevent pirating.

    Hint Collaboration helps create stakeholders.

11. The more a company depends on collaborative agreements, the more likely it is to gain control over decisions.

    Hint Collaboration assumes shared control.

12. Finding suppliers for foreign franchises can be very difficult and expensive.

    Hint McDonald's had to help farmers develop potato production to meet the standard for its fries in Thailand.

13. Turnkey operations require that keys be used to secure IPRs.

    Hint Consider the concept of giving control to a client after completing the requested project.

14. By sharing the assets with another company, one company may lose some control over the quality of its assets' use.

    Hint Shared responsibility results in a loss of control.

15. Management contracts are a means to secure foreign income without capital outlay.

    Hint Management contracts are service contracts.

MULTIPLE CHOICE

1. A strategic alliance can best be described as a relationship between two or more partners that:

   Hint An alliance assumes benefits.

   a. is of strategic importance to all parties involved.
   b. is of importance to both home- and host-country governments.
   c. is of strategic importance to at least one of the parties involved.
   d. All of the above are correct.

2. For company to contract for work with another company, one would assume that:

   Hint Contracts tend to consider segments of work.

   a. there are small volumes of business.
   b. there are highly secure portions of work.
   c. the firm has excess capacity.
   d. Companies do not contract out work.

3. The resource-based view of the firm holds that:

Hint   Know-how is the chief asset of a company.

a.   resources can be obtained easily in foreign countries.
b.   each company has a unique combination of competencies.
c.   companies must seek resources to survive.
d.   There is no resource-based view.

4. There are potential cost savings and supply assurances from vertical integration. However, companies may lack _____ or _____ to own and manage the full value chain of activities.

Hint   Companies attempt to find what is lacking.

a.   initiative; resources
b.   There are no cost savings from vertical integration.
c.   horizontal links; human resources
d.   competence; resources

5. The more a company depends on collaborative arrangements, the more likely it is to:

Hint   Collaborative arrangements require monitoring.

a.   reduce the risks.
b.   be successful.
c.   gain control.
d.   lose control over decisions.

6. A licensing agreement:

Hint   A license gives certain rights.

a.   grants rights to intangible property to another company to use in a specified geographic area for a specified period.
b.   allows for unlimited use by the licensee.
c.   is used only in countries where pirating exists.
d.   is only used for franchising globally.

7. _____ is a specialized form of licensing, which includes use of intangible property and operational assistant.

Hint   This concept is popular in the fast-food industry.

a.   Turnkey operations
b.   Franchising
c.   Management contract
d.   This type of agreement does not exist.

8. When entering foreign countries, franchisers may encounter difficulties in transferring:

Hint   Franchisers may not adjust to the foreign market.

a.   home-country employees and standardized products and services.
b.   name identification, effective cost controls, and home-country currencies.
c.   product and service standardization, name identification, and effective cost controls.
d.   Franchisers do not encounter difficulties in foreign countries.

9. With _____ _____, there are contracts that may provide a host country with assistance for a limited time period.

   Hint   Host countries may invest in buying know-how.

   a.   franchising operations
   b.   management contracts
   c.   turnkey operations
   d.   licensing contracts

10. _____ _____ are a type of collaborative arrangement in which one company contracts another to build complete, ready-to-operate facilities.

   Hint   Consider that when completed, the new owners are provided with the key to operate the new facility.

   a.   Turnkey operations
   b.   Management contracts
   c.   Construction arrangements
   d.   These types of arrangements are not allowed because of differences in engineering standards.

11. If within a collaborative arrangement at least one of the collaborating companies takes an ownership position in the others', this is referred to as:

   Hint   Ownership results in equity.

   a.   a consortium.
   b.   a joint venture.
   c.   an inequity position.
   d.   equity alliance.

12. In a collaborative arrangement, when control is ceded to one of the partners:

   Hint   Partners share accountability.

   a.   only the partner in the host country is accountable.
   b.   only the person who has control is accountable.
   c.   control is always equally distributed.
   d.   both may be held responsible.

INTERNET EXERCISES

Exercise 1.
Grupo Industrial Alfa S.A.
http://www.salidas.com.mx/ejemplos/Alfa_OLD/
Learn about this organization by going to the links within this Web site. You can click on the English icon to view the sites in English. How does this company compare with the opening Alfa case in the book? How has it changed? Write a brief essay describing your impression of Grupo Alfa at this point in time and relate it to the Chapter 14 material.

Exercise 2.
Domino's Pizza
http://www.dominos.com/
Learn about this company and its locations. Then click on the Franchising Opportunities link and go to International Franchising. What is Domino's policy towards International Franchising? Discuss in a brief essay and relate it to the concepts on franchising in Chapter 14.

Exercise 3.
Pronuptia
http://www.pronuptia.co.uk/
Read about their product line and franchising opportunities. What is this company's history and where are its branches?
Describe this company as a franchising opportunity.

Exercise 4.
Fluor Corporation
http://www.fluor.com
Familiarize yourself with this company's history and mission. How does this company conduct itself in the world of
international business? What are its products or services? Relate this company's activities to the turnkey operation
concept. How does it fit as a turnkey operation? Explain and relate to Chapter 14.

Exercise 5.
International Air Transportation Association (IATA)
http://www.iata.org
Learn about this global organization. Who are its members? What are its products and services? How does this
organization represent global cooperation? Discuss your views and assess the value of this organization.

CHAPTER 14 ANSWER KEY

True/False

1. **True** Yes, Alfa is seasoned and effective in operating in the Mexican environment.
    Difficulty: moderate
    Topic: Case: Grupo Industrial Alfa S.A. (GIASA)

2. **True** Yes, Mexican companies often have joint ventures with foreign companies who produce in Mexico and use the foreign partner's trademark to help gain customer acceptance of the Mexican output.
    Difficulty: moderate
    Topic: Case: Grupo Industrial Alfa S.A. (GIASA)

3. **False** Yes, it is false to state that companies are limited in the number of production sites they have around the world.
    Difficulty: moderate
    Topic: Introduction

4. **True** Yes, strategic alliances are formed to secure long-term goals for one or both partners.
    Difficulty: hard
    Topic: Introduction

5. **False** Yes, it is not correct to assume that McDonald's limits its franchising operations to the home market.
    Difficulty: moderate
    Topic: Motives for Collaborative Arrangements

6. **False** Yes, on the contrary, companies with excess production or sales capacity may find lucrative sources with foreign partners who have shortages.
    Difficulty: hard
    Topic: Spread and Reduce Costs

7. **False** Yes, rather than having too many product lines, companies tend to realign their product lines to focus on their major strengths.
    Difficulty: moderate
    Topic: Specialize in Competencies

8. **True** Yes, collusion is tolerated in most countries.
    Difficulty: moderate
    Topic: Avoid Competition

9. **True** Yes, cultural, political, and economic differences create barriers for foreign companies, and local partners tend to have greater ability to overcome these barriers.
    Difficulty: hard
    Topic: Gain Location-Specific Assets

10. **True** Yes, a foreign company may seek local partners to create stakeholders who will provide protection against IPR pirating.
    Difficulty: moderate
    Topic: Overcome Legal Constraints

11. **False** Yes, it is wrong to assume that collaborative agreements enhance a company's control over decisions. The tendency is for the opposite to occur.
    Difficulty: easy
    Topic: Some Considerations in Collaborative Arrangements

12. True   Yes, supplies can be hard to find or nonexistent, in which case they have to be created.
      Difficulty: moderate
      Topic: Operational Modifications

13. False   No, the concept of turnkey suggests that a company releases the "key" to a project when it is finished creating it for another company.
      Difficulty: hard
      Topic: Turnkey Operations

14. True   Yes, an example is the marketing strategy of a perfume company that diminished the image of another company's product line by introducing the product to discount stores.
      Difficulty: moderate
      Topic: Control Problems

15. True   Yes, management contracts provide management know-how and tend to have minimal capital outlay.
      Difficulty: hard
      Topic: Summary

Multiple Choice

1. c.   Yes, a strategic alliance must be of strategic importance to at least one of the partners if it is to be considered strategic.
      Difficulty: moderate
      Topic: Introduction

2. a.   Yes, contractors tend to get small parts of a company's work that is outsourced.
      Difficulty: moderate
      Topic: Motives for Collaborative Arrangements: General

3. b.   Yes, competencies are the resource in the resource-based view.
      Difficulty: moderate
      Topic: Specialize in Competencies

4. d.   Yes a company may lack the competence or resources to take advantage of vertical integration.
      Difficulty: moderate
      Topic: Secure Vertical and Horizontal Links

5. d.   Yes, companies who depend on collaborative arrangements tend to have less control over quality in output, new product directions, and where to expand markets.
      Difficulty: moderate
      Topic: Some Considerations in Collaborative Arrangements

6. a.   Yes, this correctly describes a licensing agreement.
      Difficulty: easy
      Topic: Licensing

7. b.   Yes, franchising is a specialized form of licensing in which the franchiser not only sells an independent franchisee the use of intangible property such as a trademark, but also provides operational assistance on a continuous basis.
      Difficulty: easy
      Topic: Franchising

8. c. Yes, these are areas that may be taken for granted in the home country, but may not easily transfer to a host country.
    Difficulty: hard
    Topic: Operational Modification

9. b. Yes, management contracts tend to be for a short period such as three or five years and provide experienced management talent from a foreign company, usually for a fixed fee.
    Difficulty: moderate
    Topic: Management Contracts

10. a. Yes, the above statement describes a turnkey operation.
    Difficulty: easy
    Topic: Turnkey Operations

11. d. Yes, an equity alliance occurs when collaborative relationships also result in one or more partners taking an ownership position in the venture.
    Difficulty: hard
    Topic: Equity Alliances

12. d. Yes, legal systems and circumstances may hold both parties responsible, even if one party has ceded control to the other.
    Difficulty: moderate
    Topic: Control Problems

Chapter 15

Control Strategies

CHAPTER OBJECTIVES

1. To explain the special challenges of controlling foreign operations.

2. To describe organizational structures for international operations.

3. To show the advantages and disadvantages of decision making at headquarters and at foreign subsidiary locations.

4. To highlight both the importance of and the method for global planning, reporting, and evaluating.

5. To give an overview of some specific control considerations affecting MNEs, such as the handling of acquisitions and the shifts in strategies to fulfill international objectives.

TRUE/FALSE

1. Nestlé's corporate management handles all acquisition decisions at its headquarters in Switzerland.

    Hint   Control is centralized at Nestlé's.

2. Nestlé's country managers have a great deal of discretion.

    Hint   Nestlé's products need to be differentiated according to consumer taste preferences.

3. Nestlé's control policy is too keep managers focused on one territory rather than rotate them into other areas.

    Hint   Nestlé's wants its managers to have a conceptual overview of the whole corporation.

4. Top management's control strategy focuses mainly on securing enough voting shares to direct company policy.

    Hint   Control strategies for international operations are complex.

5. Nestlé's managers consider cost to be the most important criteria for control.

    Hint   Nestlé's major competitive advantage lies in marketing differentiated consumer products.

6. Distance is a factor that makes control more difficult internationally.

    Hint   Distance includes time zones and geographic distance.

7. When a company adapts its resources and objectives to changing international markets, it tends to do so quickly and sporadically rather than to use extensive planning techniques.

    Hint   Planning is an essential element of managerial control.

8. A company establishes its overall rationale for international activities by doing an internal analysis.

    Hint   An internal analysis considers internal corporate resources.

9. International companies should refrain from setting specific objectives for each subsidiary.

   Hint   Objectives provide guidelines for assessments.

10. Uncertainties in the international sphere do not create additional difficulties for planners.

    Hint   Complexities make planning more difficult.

11. International division structures are used more often by U.S. MNEs than European MNEs.

    Hint   An international division tends to rely on its domestic division.

12. A matrix organization is considered the best structure for MNEs.

    Hint   Matrix organizations have a dual-reporting system.

13. A significant component of establishing organizational structures is the fact that decision makers are clearly identified.

    Hint   The complexities of decision making increases with MNEs.

14. The higher the pressure for global integration, the greater the need to centralize decision making.

    Hint   Global integration requires a main focus.

15. By placing foreign personnel on the board of directors and top-level committees, MNEs seek to coordinate functions.

    Hint   Directors bring in other viewpoints to top-level decisions.

MULTIPLE CHOICE

1. The budgets that originate from Nestlé in each country ensure that:

   Hint   Budgets monitor productivity.

   a.   the company meets operational commitments.
   b.   each country carries its share in the corporation.
   c.   budgets are not decentralized.
   d.   there are no losses.

2. To control its international business, Nestlé relies:

   Hint   Control methods are varied.

   a.   heavily on information obtained from directors appointed from foreign locations.
   b.   exclusively on monitoring budgets.
   c.   heavily on budgets and reports and information from foreign operations.
   d.   heavily on outside consultants.

3.   For MNEs, control requires that management:

Hint   Control is a company's strategy to keep on track.

   a.   have reliable supervisors.
   b.   do planning, operating, and supervising.
   c.   implement a micromanagement strategy and have yearly audits.
   d.   engage in planning, implementing of plans, evaluation, and correction of performance standards that do not meet the set objectives.

4.   The Barings bank collapse is an example of:

Hint   Barings bank allowed a futures trader a great amount of freedom.

   a.   a weak control system in the bank.
   b.   a bank that had marginal operating success.
   c.   excessive competition.
   d.   a government shutdown.

5.   The first step in a company's international planning process is to:

Hint   Planning projects into the future.

   a.   develop a long-range strategic intent.
   b.   start exporting.
   c.   implement strategy.
   d.   Both (a) and (c) are correct.

6.   Because each country in which a company is planning to operate in is unique, managers should _____ and _____.

Hint   Companies need to consider diverse issues.

   a.   analyze local conditions; implement strategy
   b.   avoid unique countries; go with the familiar
   c.   analyze local conditions; select alternatives based on those conditions
   d.   Countries are not considered unique from a planning perspective because each country has the same basic infrastructure.

7.   The difference between strategic plans and operating plans is:

Hint   Think long term versus short term.

   a.   operation plans suggest long-term operations and strategic plans suggest short-term considerations.
   b.   strategic plans are futuristic and long term, whereas operating plans formulate short-term objectives and operating processes.
   c.   strategic plans are created for external operations, and operating plans are created for internal operations.
   d.   There is no difference between the two terms; they can be used interchangeably.

8. When all of a company's foreign subsidiaries report to one department that is responsible for the company's international business, the company is using:

Hint   Consider that the one department is channeling all international business transactions.

   a.   an international division structure.
   b.   a functional division structure.
   c.   a geographic division.
   d.   matrix structure.

9. A geographic division structure is common to:

Hint   Geographic divisions tend to represent clusters of countries in a particular region.

   a.   U.S. MNEs.
   b.   all MNEs because it is the most efficient organizational structure for international business.
   c.   European MNEs.
   d.   Geographic structures are rarely used.

10. The Japanese keiretsu network may best be described as:

Hint   Japanese culture values interrelationships.

   a.   a series of theater restaurants catering to businesspeople.
   b.   a network of companies in which each owns a small percentage of other companies in the network.
   c.   a distribution system initiated by the Japanese government.
   d.   a vertically integrated system.

11. Decisions makers are aware that pricing and product decisions in one country:

Hint   Sourcing for industrial and consumer products is done worldwide.

   a.   can affect demand in other countries.
   b.   only affects domestic demand.
   c.   are easily established when based on per capita income figures.
   d.   fluctuates with that country's currency.

12. Companies that are ideal candidates for transnational strategies are companies that:

Hint   Industries that use transnational strategies include pharmaceutical and computer companies.

   a.   focus on global integration.
   b.   have local responsiveness and global integration.
   c.   have local responsiveness.
   d.   are in the transportation business.

13. Upper management's perception of the competence of corporate versus local managers will:

Hint   Competencies are critical in business decisions.

   a.   influence the location of decision making.
   b.   always choose corporate managers to maintain control.
   c.   be driven by local politics.
   d.   Upper managers will always choose from among their own ranks.

14. Branch operations are possible only if:

Hint   Branches are part of one entity and do not stand alone.

   a.   they are in the same country.
   b.   the parent holds 100% ownership.
   c.   it is legally separate from the parent company.
   d.   they are located in the same city as the parent company.

15. A fundamental difference between GE's culture and the Tungsram culture was based in:

Hint   In the United States, individuals believe that outside constraints can be overcome.

   a.   the U.S. belief that obstacles are insurmountable and the Hungarian belief that fate directed one's destiny.
   b.   the U. S. personnel's focus was inner-directed and believed that it is up to each individual to overcome outside constraints, whereas the Hungarians were outer-directed and believed that individuals could not overcome outside forces.
   c.   There were no cultural differences.
   d.   religious dogma.

INTERNET EXERCISES

Exercise 1.
Nestlé
http://www.nestle.com
Link to their worldwide addresses. How does this company represent itself globally? How does the Web site reflect Nestlé's control strategy as discussed in the case? Describe.

Exercise 2.
GE Lighting
http://www.gelighting.com
Study how this company is organized. Relate your findings to the discussion on organizational structure in Chapter 15 in a brief essay.

Exercise 3.
OSRAM
http://www.osram.com and http://www.gelighting.com
Familiarize yourself with this company's diverse locations. Compare this company's organizational structure to the GE Lighting site. How are these companies different and how are they the same? Consider their organizational structure and similar products and services in light of the discussion on control strategies in Chapter 15.

Exercise 4.
Prudential Web
http://www.prudential.com and http://www.nestle.com
Compare to the Nestlé site and study each company's sites in Asia. Do you agree that the Prudential operations are more autonomous that the Nestlé operations? If so, why, if not, why not?

Exercise 5.
Canon
http://www.canon.com
Consider the concept of strategic intent and explore the Canon Web site with this in mind. How does Canon position itself to reflect strategic intent? Discuss.

CHAPTER 15 ANSWER KEY

True/False

1. a.   Yes, to maintain control, Nestlé's at its headquarters in Switzerland handles all acquisition decisions as well as those regarding which products it will research.
        Difficulty: easy
        Topic: Case: Nestlé

2. a.   Yes, although Nestlé's decision making is centralized, country managers have a great deal of discretion in matters such as product changes to fit local preferences and in marketing strategies.
        Difficulty: moderate
        Topic: Case: Nestlé

3. b.   Yes, rather than isolating managers in one particular area, Nestlé's prefers to rotate them to other sites so that they become familiar with the total concept of the company.
        Difficulty: moderate
        Topic: Case: Nestlé.

4. b.   Yes, the concept of control is more complex and requires that top management focus on planning, implementation, evaluation, and correction of performance to ensure that the organization meets its objectives.
        Difficulty: moderate
        Topic: Introduction

5. b.   No, it is not correct to assume that costs are the most critical control factor. Proper alignment of Nestlé's product line to local markets is the most important criteria for control.
        Difficulty: hard
        Topic: Introduction

6. a.   Yes, although there have been vast improvements in communications and transportation, the best interactions for control purposes tend to still be face-to-face.
        Difficulty: easy
        Topic: Introduction

7. b.   Yes, it is false to assume that managers tend to sporadically react to the environment rather than exercise the planning process.
        Difficulty: moderate
        Topic: Planning

8. a.   Yes, an internal analysis considers the critical resources of a company and includes: financial resources, human resources, product resources, and environmental effects on those resources.
        Difficulty: moderate
        Topic: The Planning Loop

9. b.   Yes, it is not correct to state the specific objectives for subsidiaries should not be required because objectives help in assessments and control strategies.
        Difficulty: moderate
        Topic: Planning Loop

10. b.   Uncertainties challenge the planning process.
        Difficulty: easy
        Topic: Uncertainty and Planning

11. a.   Yes, U.S.-based MNEs tend to use the international division structure because domestic markets establish a good support base for this type of structure.
     Difficulty: hard
     Topic: International Division Structure

12. b.   Matrix organizations have numerous drawbacks, and the most serious of these is the dual-reporting system inherent in this structure that tends to blur accountability.
     Difficulty: hard
     Topic: Matrix Division Structure

13. b.   Yes, the location of decision making may vary within the same company over time as well as by product, function, and country.
     Difficulty: hard
     Topic: Location of Decision Making

14   a.   Yes, global integration will require a centralized approach to gain consensus
     Difficulty: hard
     Topic: Pressures for Global Integration versus Local Responsiveness

15. a.   Yes, this method may be used to develop mechanisms to pull together the diverse international perspectives.
     Difficulty: hard
     Topic: Coordinating Methods

Multiple Choice

1   b   Yes, budgets are carefully scrutinized to ensure that performance standards are met for each country.
     Difficulty: moderate
     Topic: Case: Nestlé.

2.   c.   Yes, Nestlé's uses a number of control functions such as traditional budgets and reports and also makes a point of visiting foreign operations to scan for opportunities as well as to gather important assessment information.
     Difficulty: moderate
     Topic: Case: Nestlé

3.   d.   Yes, this process describes the concept of control that MNEs need to engage in to meet strategic objectives.
     Difficulty: hard
     Topic: Introduction

4.   a.   Yes, this British investment bank collapsed because there was no clear-cut control policy regarding the amount of risks that could be taken.
     Difficulty: moderate
     Topic: Introduction

5.   a.   Yes, the international planning process initially establishes a long-term objective that guides its tactical strategies.
     Difficulty: moderate
     Topic: Planning

6.   c.   Yes, managers need to analyze and become familiar with local conditions and carefully select and prioritize strategies based on their findings before implementing their plans.
     Difficulty: moderate
     Topic: Planning

7. b.   Yes, this is the correct response.
    Difficulty: moderate
    Topic: Planning

8. a.   Yes, this correctly describes an international division structure.
    Difficulty: hard
    Topic: Organizational Structure

9. c.   Yes, companies such as Nestlé that is based in Switzerland uses the geographic division structure by
            segmenting territories into geographic clusters.
    Difficulty: hard
    Topic: Organizational Structure

10. b.   Yes, this succinctly describes the Japanese keiretsu.
    Difficulty: moderate
    Topic: Network Organizations

11. a.   Yes, because of advances in transportation and communication, it is now possible to source products
            from other countries if the product or price in a specific country is preferred.
    Difficulty: moderate
    Topic: Systematic Dealings with Stakeholders

12. b.   Yes, this fits the transnational strategy and incorporates both a global and multidomestic profile.
    Difficulty: moderate
    Topic: Transnational Strategy

13. a.   Local managers may be chosen for their competences as well as to enhance morale.
    Difficulty: easy
    Topic: Capabilities of Headquarters versus Subsidiary Personnel

14. b.   Yes, this succinctly describes a branch operation.
    Difficulty: moderate
    Topic: Branch and Subsidiary Structures

15. b.   Yes, this describes the key differences in perceptions between the GE and the Tungsram employees,
            and this difference in attitude affected each party's approach to problem solving.
    Difficulty: hard
    Topic: Case: GE's Tungsram Acquisition

Chapter 16

Marketing

CHAPTER OBJECTIVES

1. To introduce techniques for assessing market sizes for given countries.

2. To describe a range of product policies and the circumstances in which they are appropriate.

3. To contrast practices of standardized versus differentiated marketing programs for each country in which sales are made.

4. To emphasize how environmental differences complicate the management of marketing worldwide.

5. To discuss the major international considerations within the marketing mix: product, pricing, promotion, branding, and distribution.

TRUE/FALSE

1. Although Avon's foreign markets have expanded considerably; its strongest growth potential is still in the United States.

   Hint   About 5% of the world's women live in the United States and Canada.

2. A lack of infrastructure in foreign locations provides ideal marketing opportunities for Avon.

   Hint   Avon products are frequently sold from door-to-door.

3. Avon's advantage in the global market is that the company standardizes its product lines.

   Hint   Avon gears its products to specific markets.

4. There is a spin-off effect from Avon's differentiation strategy.

   Hint   Processes can be adapted.

5. Avon's door-to-door sales in China have increased since 1998.

   Hint   China has laws regulating to-do-door canvassing.

6. Consumers in emerging economies always follow the same patterns as those in higher income countries.

   Hint   Consider the concept of leapfrogging.

7. Income elasticity varies by product and income level.

   Hint   Consider the difference in survival products and discretionary products.

8. Where income equality is high, per capita GNP figures tend to be low.

   Hint   Income inequality tends to represent many people who have little income.

9.	Marketers need to know that countries with similar per capita GNP have similar preferences for products because of their purchasing power.

	Hint	Cultural and regional differences dictate taste.

10.	A gap analysis can only be used in the domestic market.

	Hint	A gap analysis is a method for estimating a company's potential sales by identifying market segments it is not serving.

11.	Heineken has needed to forego markets such as Saudi Arabia because beer is not allowed there.

	Hint	Heineken adapts its products to suit local needs.

12.	A foreign country's legal requirements can dictate product alteration.

	Hint	Laws vary in different countries regarding product safety.

13.	Product alterations are cheap and should always be made to meet foreign market requirements.

	Hint	Cost comparisons should be made before costs are incurred.

14.	A skimming strategy uses a low introductory price to induce maximum sales.

	Hint	Skimming connotes skimming rich cream off the top.

15.	Government regulations may directly or indirectly affect the prices a company charges.

	Hint	Government regulations are legal mandates and require conformity.

MULTIPLE CHOICE

1.	The Avon company is headquartered in the United States but:

	Hint	Avon has a significant presence in foreign countries.

	a.	25% of its sales are outside the United States.
	b.	50% of its employees are in foreign countries.
	c.	about 65% of is sales its and 75% of its employees are outside of the United States.
	d.	it has FDI in 20 countries.

2.	Avon often uses English or French brand names abroad because:

	Hint	Brand names create images.

	a.	Avon only sells in English- and French-speaking countries.
	b.	consumers consider English and French brand names of high quality.
	c.	instructions in these languages are easy to read.
	d.	Avon only uses American/English brand names.

3. Avon runs a new campaign with price adjustments every two to three weeks that:

   Hint   Economic factors can impact prices.

   a.   allows for seasonal promotions.
   b.   allows for inventory control.
   c.   Avon does not adjust its prices very often.
   d.   is helpful for adjusting prices in highly inflationary economies.

4. Avon's focus on support for women includes a major social responsibility project internationally in fighting:

   Hint   Avon promotes health awareness for women.

   a.   breast cancer.
   b.   civil war.
   c.   the discrimination towards women.
   d.   Avon does not get involved with programs that target women.

5. A _____ _____ is a tool to help estimate why sales are less than the potential for all competitors in the country.

   Hint   Consider the line between what is and what could be.

   a.   gap analysis
   b.   benchmarking
   c.   Marketers do not use tools. Marketing is an intuitive process.
   d.   distribution gap

6. _____ gaps are gaps that indicate that consumers are not using the amount of a product that was expected.

   Hint   This gap may exist if customers are not familiar with the product.

   a.   Lost
   b.   Usage
   c.   Distribution
   d.   Marketers cannot anticipate use of a product.

7. A company that places serious consideration on potential environmental, health, social, and work-related problems when selling abroad is considered to have a _____ marketing orientation:

   Hint   The above factors consider the social fabric in marketing.

   a.   legal
   b.   societal
   c.   Companies do not consider these factors; their main concern is to generate a profit.
   d.   environmental

8. A company that offers discounts through coupons and box top specials in Germany must:

   Hint   Government regulations in Germany monitor giveaways.

   a.   reduce the product price at a consistent percentage.
   b.   have a consistent policy regarding these promotions throughout the year.
   c.   pay a fine to the government.
   d.   Coupons and discounts are not used in Germany.

9. The gray market is a phenomenon that occurs when:

   Hint Gray markets are unofficial and illegal in many countries.

   a. senior executives initiate price cutting.
   b. goods are sold damaged.
   c. consumers buy a good abroad at a cheaper price than what this good is sold for at home and then imports this item.
   d. Both (a) and (b) are correct.

10. Generally, the more _____ _____the distribution system, the more likely a company is to emphasize a push strategy.

    Hint Push strategies are personalized promotion strategies.

    a. tightly controlled
    b. loosely controlled.
    c. There is no real relationships between distributions systems and push or pull strategies.
    d. pull in

11. Standardized advertising usually means:

    Hint Consider culture and language in advertising globally.

    a. a program that is similar from market to market rather than identical.
    b. creating identical ads.
    c. It is not possible to standardize advertising.
    d. the same actors are used with foreign languages dubbed in.

12. Legal advertising in each country is:

    Hint Laws and customs are similar as well as different from country to country.

    a. based on WTO mandates.
    b. clearly documented by advertising professionals.
    c. similar and follows the British system.
    d. based on varying national views on consumer protection standards of morality and nationalism.

13. MNEs find distribution one of the most difficult functions to standardize internationally because:

    Hint Distribution systems are evolutionary.

    a. corruption runs rampant within distributions systems.
    b. distribution systems are entwined in cultural, economic, and legal environments.
    c. MNEs do not find distributions systems internationally a difficult function.
    d. distribution systems are not technically linked.

14. The major problems for standardizing advertising in different countries are:

    Hint Diversity makes standardization difficult.

    a. translation, legality, and message needs.
    b. a lack of advertising agencies.
    c. There are no problems with standardizing advertising in different countries.
    d. Both (a) and (b) are correct.

15. *Dental News* marketing strategies target _____

    Hint   *Dental News* seeks to bring information to less-developed markets.

    a.   Triad markets because they are more lucrative.
    b.   *Dental News* does not have a specific target market.
    c.   non-Triad markets.
    d.   the Japanese market.

INTERNET EXERCISES

Exercise 1.
Avon
http://www.avon.com
Get an overview of the company, its history, and the emphasis it places on women. Describe this company's business philosophy and focus on women. Write a brief summary that discusses Avon's business strategy as a marketing concept.

Exercise 2.Avon
http://www.avon.com
Explore the Global directory by accessing "Avon Around the World. Explore each continent category listed, access one country within each continent, and consider Avon's marketing strategy in that country. Suggestion: Compare countries such as Brazil, Germany, and Russia to get a mix of developing and developed markets. Discuss the different approaches Avon uses in these countries.

Exercise 3.
Heineken
http://www.Heineken.com
Explore the beer and bar sites of the global network. Enter bars around the globe by clicking on "quick and easy registration" and provide the necessary information to enter the Heineken global bar environment. Describe your findings by discussing Heineken's target market and strategy in establishing a global image.

Exercise 4.
Tyson Foods, Inc.
http://www.tyson.com
Explore the Web site and familiarize yourself with the company by linking to their international sites. Then go back to the main site and read at least three news articles that discuss Tyson's programs regarding food safety, workplace safety, etc. Then briefly describe Tyson societal marketing orientation as discussed in Chapter 16.

Exercise 5.
Dental News
http://www.dentalnews.com
Describe this company and its marketing orientation in a brief essay.

CHAPTER 16 ANSWER KEY

True/False

1. b. Avon's potential in foreign markets exceeds that of the U.S. because of the sheer size of the market outside of the U.S.
   Difficulty: easy
   Topic: Case: Avon

2. a. Yes, Avon representatives go directly to the consumer rather than the consumer needing to traverse difficult terrain to go to shopping districts to purchase Avon's products.
   Difficulty: moderate
   Topic: Case: Avon

3. b. Yes, it is false to assume that Avon sells the same product line to all countries. Instead, Avon differentiates its product line from country to country and considers local needs and preferences.
   Difficulty: moderate
   Topic: Case: Avon

4. a. Yes, Avon may adapt production processes or preferred product lines to be used in other countries.
   Difficulty: hard
   Topic: Case: Avon

5. b. Yes, on the contrary, Avon has opened retail stores in China in response to the law forbidding door-to-door sales.
   Difficulty: moderate
   Topic: Case: Avon

6. b. Yes it is not correct to assume that consumers follow the same patterns in a developing country as consumers have in the industrialized nations. Instead, newly emerging countries may leapfrog or jump over certain steps with new technologies, such as is the case with the cell phone.
   Difficulty: moderate
   Topic: Total Market Potential

7. a. Yes, for example, demand for food is usually less elastic that demand for optional items such as an automobile or products of enhancement.
   Difficulty: hard
   Topic: Income Elasticity

8. a. Yes, in countries where a small percentage of the population has a high income and the rest are poor, this would reduce the per capita GNP figures even though an upper- and middle-income bracket also exists in that country.
   Difficulty: moderate
   Topic: Income Inequality

9. b. Yes, is not correct to assume that consumers have similar or the same preference in products because they are at similar income levels. Personal preference and choice varies among domestic and foreign consumers.
   Difficulty: easy
   Topic: Cultural Factors and Taste

10. b. Yes, it is false to assume that companies are limited in using a gap analysis for domestic markets only.
    Difficulty: easy
    Topic: Gap Analysis

11.   b.   Although Heineken does not actively pursue every market in the world, it does market its products in alcohol-free countries such as Saudi Arabia and has introduced a nonalcoholic drink similar to beer, but called malt.
      Difficulty: moderate
      Topic: Strategic Marketing Orientation

12.   a.   Yes, in addition to consumer preferences, a county's legal mandates may require product alterations.
      Difficulty: moderate
      Topic: Reasons for Product Alteration

13.   b.   Alterations may or may not be inexpensive. The cost of the alterations should be considered along with the potential from sales revenue to offset these costs.
      Difficulty: moderate
      Topic: Alteration Costs

14.   b.   Low introductory prices are part of a penetration strategy not skimming strategy.
      Difficulty: moderate
      Topic: Greater Market Diversity

15.   a.   Yes, government regulations are diverse and may be in the form of tariffs, product redesign, or the use of a distribution chain or operation procedure and can add direct as well as indirect costs to a product or service.
      Difficulty: moderate
      Topic: Summary

Multiple Choice

1.   c.   Yes, Avon has a large presence outside of the United States.
      Difficulty: hard
      Topic: Case: Avon

2.   b.   Yes, English and French names have a high image for beauty products for most consumers.
      Difficulty: moderate
      Topic: Case: Avon

3.   d.   Yes, a policy of frequent promotions price adjustments creates a natural opportunity to adjust to specific inflationary or other economic trends in certain countries.
      Difficulty: hard
      Topic: Case: Avon

4.   a.   Yes, Avon disseminates information about breast cancer along with their promotional brochures and sells pins to raise money for local needs.
      Difficulty: moderate
      Topic: Case: Avon

5.   a.   Yes, a gap analysis is a method for estimating a company's potential sales by identifying market segments it is not serving adequately.
      Difficulty: moderate
      Topic: Gap Analysis

6. b.   Yes, usage gaps reflect a lack of sales where sales had been anticipated. An example would be that in some countries chocolate is not a familiar taste, and the majority of the population do not eat chocolate. Hence, chocolate confections may not be a popular purchase until a company promotes the use of chocolate.
       Difficulty: moderate
       Topic: Gap Analysis

7. b.   Yes, companies with a societal marketing orientation will consider the above factors when selling or marketing their products abroad.
       Difficulty: moderate
       Topic: Societal Marketing Orientation

8. b.   Yes, the German government does not encourage coupons or other promotional giveaways and requires that companies who use this promotion strategy have a consistent giveaway policy throughout the year.
       Difficulty: hard
       Topic: Governmental Interventions

9. c.   Yes, an example of this type of transaction is if a Korean purchases an automobile abroad and imports it at a cheaper price than what the local distributor is charging.
       Difficulty: moderate
       Topic: Currency Value and Price Changes

10. a.   Yes, a tightly controlled distribution system requires greater effort to get distributors to handle a product.
       Difficulty: hard
       Topic: The Push-Pull Mix

11. a.   Yes, standardized advertising focuses on key concepts, but still allows for local language and cultural considerations.
       Difficulty: moderate
       Topic: Standardization of Advertising Programs

12. d.   Yes, companies must be aware of the value base within each country's legal system that is unique to that country.
       Difficulty: moderate
       Topic: Standardization of Advertising Programs

13. b.   Yes, distribution systems are complex and are deeply entrenched in local custom and often represent fundamental relationship ties among the business community.
       Difficulty: hard
       Topic: Difficulty of Standardization

14. a.   Yes, it is difficult to standardize advertising when the standards from country to country are different.
       Difficulty: easy
       Topic: Summary

15. c.   Yes, by focusing on markets other than the Triad countries, *Dental News* believes that they will reach potential customers who have little access to information.
       Difficulty: hard
       Topic: Case: *Dental News* and Hotresponse

Chapter 17

Export and Import Strategies

CHAPTER OBJECTIVES

1. To identify the key elements of export and import strategies.

2. To compare direct and indirect selling of exports.

3. To discuss the role of several types of trading companies in exporting.

4. To show how freight forwarders help exporters and the financing of receivables.

5. To discuss the role of countertrade in international business.

TRUE/FALSE

1. The president of Grieve Corporation found that Asian customers prefer to deal with top managers.

   Hint   Asian customers tend to establish personal associations with key decision makers.

2. Exporting requires a lower level of investment than other modes of reaching foreign markets.

   Hint   Exporting tends to be a low-risk entry mode to foreign trade.

3. Internalization advantages come from licensing assets or skills.

   Hint   Internalization means holding onto and integrating assets.

4. Exporting is always a benefit to the exporting company.

   Hint   Companies consider costs and benefits when undertaking a new strategy.

5. Export diversification can allow a company to balance markets.

   Hint   Markets fluctuate.

6. Many companies begin exporting by accident rather than by design.

   Hint   Exports may be initiated by an unsolicited request for a product.

7. An unwillingness to modify products for export is among a list of reasons why companies fail in exporting.

   Hint   Countries have specific regulations and cultural preferences for products and services.

8. There are virtually no guidelines to export transactions because of the nature of the process.

   Hint   Consider the international business transaction chain.

9. For U.S. companies the best place to start to obtain export counseling is with the ITA.

   Hint   The U.S. Department of Commerce has established Export Assistance Centers as part of the International Trade Administration.

10. The import process should not be confused with the export process because they are opposites.

   Hint   Importing and exporting are similar and different.

11. Exporting may be either direct or indirect.

   Hint   There are various ways to reach a customer.

12. A freight forwarder may be used for both imports and exports.

   Hint   Freight forwarders are known as the travel agents of cargo.

13. Export licenses are generally licenses and merely require consistent and methodical documentation.

   Hint   In the United States there are two types of export licenses.

14. Letters of credit are safer because they are always irrevocable.

   Hint   There are different types of conditions for letters of credit.

15. Countertrade can be either bilateral or multilateral arrangements.

   Hint   Countertrade can take many directions.

MULTIPLE CHOICE

1. Grieve Corporation learned some valuable lessons about exporting and recommended nine strategies. One of the strategies not recommended was:

   Hint   Grieve Corporation recommended good business strategies.

   a.   learn the customs and business etiquette of the countries you visit.
   b.   learn more about the competition and the potential sales for your product.
   c.   see the sights and relax; balance your trip with equal work and play.
   d.   have a principal contact at the home office to answer questions and provide assistance.

2. A company's choice of entry mode to a foreign market depends on factors such as:

   Hint   A company needs to consider strategic goals.

   a.   government support and currency fluctuations.
   b.   ownership advantage, location advantage, and internalization advantage.
   c.   ownership advantage overall.
   d.   home-country labor unrest.

3. Researchers found two basic characteristics of exports, and they are:

   Hint   The two conclusions focus on probability and intensity.

   a.   small companies increase the probability of exporting and the greater the total revenue coming from export the greater the intensity of concentration on exports.
   b.   there is little research on what drives companies to engage in export.
   c.   the probability of being an exporter increases with company size as defined by revenue and the greater percentage a company's total revenue that is derived from export the greater the intensity the company puts on exports.
   d.   risk and industry factors were less important than the size of the company.

4. There are many potential pitfalls of exporting; however, they do not include:

   Hint   Consider what should be done instead of what should not be done.

   a.   failure to obtain qualified export counseling and to develop a master international marketing plan before starting an export business.
   b.   neglecting export business when the domestic market booms.
   c.   insufficient commitment by top management to overcome the initial difficulties and financial requirements of exporting.
   d.   establishing a base of profitable operations and orderly growth rather than chasing orders from around the world.

5. Several excellent resource pools in the United States to help determine markets to which products like its own are currently being exported can be found in:

   Hint   Governments tend to help companies with their export needs.

   a.   Department of Revenue and U.S. Census Trade Statistics.
   b.   the National Trade Data Bank (NTDB) and the U.S. Census Trade Statistics.
   c.   trade associations.
   d.   economic development councils.

6. The two basic types of imports include:

   Hint   Imports may stand alone or be connected with a strategic goal.

   a.   industrial and consumer goods and services to individuals or intermediate goods and services that are part of the firm's global supply chain.
   b.   foreign and domestic.
   c.   perishable and nonperishable.
   d.   None of the answers are correct.

7. When merchandise reaches the port of entry, the importer must:

   Hint   Consider the role of customs officials with regard to imports.

   a.   have a truck waiting to take delivery of the goods.
   b.   file the appropriate documents with customs officials, who then assign a tentative value and tariff classification to the merchandise.
   c.   take delivery of the goods.
   d.   meet the ship with the proper documentation.

8. Because governments assess duties on imports based on the country of origin, a mistake in marking the country of origin could result in:

   Hint   Customs regulations are varied and carry penalties for nonconformity.

   a.   request for a bribe.
   b.   the good being shipped back for remarking.
   c.   higher import duties.
   d.   Imported items always have the correct country of origin mark when they enter another country.

9. In the United States, the drawback provision allows domestic exporters to apply for a 99% refund of the duty paid on imported goods, as long as:

   Hint   Drawback provisions tend to be used by manufacturers who import components for goods that will be exported.

   a.   local labor is used in processing these goods.
   b.   the imported good are used for products that will be exported again.
   c.   Drawback provisions do not exist.
   d.   the items are distributed in the state where they are imported.

10. A freight forwarder is an intermediary who takes responsibility for:

    Hint   Freight forwarders are external to a company.

    a.   all aspects of imports and exports.
    b.   trucking the good from the entry port to the buyer's destination.
    c.   the packing and crating of goods.
    d.   moving the products between domestic and foreign markets.

11. A sales representative sells products in foreign markets on a commission basis, without:

    Hint   Sales representatives have limited power.

    a.   taking title to the goods.
    b.   accountability to the company.
    c.   restrictions.
    d.   considering pricing guidelines.

12. The terms sogo shosha, keiretsu, zaibatsu, and chaebol represent entities in certain historic periods and generally refer to:

    Hint   The terms refer to powerful groups within Asia.

    a.   political parties in Japan and Korea.
    b.   shipping companies.
    c.   trading companies.
    d.   a traditional ceremony to celebrate prosperity.

13. A _____ is a receipt for goods delivered to the common carrier for transportation, a contract for the services rendered by the carrier, and a document of title.

   Hint   This document is an important document in a trading transaction.

   a.   consular invoice
   b.   certificate of origin
   c.   bill of lading
   d.   No one document represents all of the functions stated in the question.

14. A preferred type of letter of credit used in trade transactions is the _____ letter of credit.

   Hint   Foreign payment forms seek to minimize risk.

   a.   revocable
   b.   irrevocable
   c.   sight
   d.   Letters of credit do not reduce payment risks.

15. Countertrade is any one of several different arrangements by which goods and services are traded. Within these arrangements the term _____ means trading goods for goods.

   Hint   This practice is used in exchange processes outside of foreign trade as well.

   a.   offset
   b.   buybacks
   c.   barter
   d.   All of the above are correct.

INTERNET EXERCISES

Exercise 1.
U.S. Department of Commerce
http://osecnt13.osec.doc.gov
Study their mission statement and the overview of various department bureaus. Click on Bureau of Acronyms and go to BXA, FCS, and ITA. Briefly describe your findings and how this information can benefit someone in international trade.

Exercise 2.
Export-Import Bank for the United States
http://www.exim.gov
Explore this site and note what services are available through this agency. Discuss how a novice in international trade may benefit by using this agency's services.

Exercise 3.
E-commerce
http://ecommerce.internet.com/ and http://www.ecommerce.gov/internat.htm
Investigate e-commerce opportunities by visiting the E-commerce Guide and the U.S. Government E-commerce policy site and get a conceptual framework of e-commerce on a global basis. Then write a succinct position paper describing e-commerce as a new opportunity for international trade.

Exercise 4.
Mitsui & Co
http://www.mitsui.co.jp
Hit "Go English" and study this trading company's industrial and product portfolio. Describe your findings and relate them to the section on trading companies and the sogo shosha. How does this company differ from the zaibatsu description? Or is it the same? Explain.

Exercise 5.
HSCB Banking
http://www.HSBC.com
Access International Networks as well as Products and Services. How can a company engaged in international trade benefit by using this bank's services? Explain.

CHAPTER 17 ANSWER KEY

True/False

1. True   Yes, Patrick Calabrese found that Asian customers are attuned to a president talking to a president and feel secure when they are dealing with someone who can make decisions.
    Difficulty: easy
    Topic: Case: Grieve Corporation: A Small Business Export Strategy

2. True   Although exporting has start-up costs as well as operating costs, it tends to require less outlay and a quicker return than other modes of reaching foreign markets.
    Difficulty: moderate
    Topic: Export Strategy

3. False   Yes, internalization does not refer to making assets or skills available to outsiders through licensing.
    Difficulty: moderate
    Topic: Export Strategy

4. False   To assume that exporting is always a benefit to a company does not consider other domestic opportunities such as expanding markets at home instead.
    Difficulty: hard
    Topic: Export Strategy

5. True   Yes, export diversification can allow a company to take advantage of strong growth in one market to offset weak growth in another market.
    Difficulty: hard
    Topic: Why Companies Export

6. True   Yes, companies may be unprepared when responding to a request for a product from abroad.
    Difficulty: moderate
    Topic: Stages of Export Development

7. True   Yes, exporting companies must consider the legal and cultural factors of the importing country and how their products or services will impact those barriers.
    Difficulty: moderate
    Topic: Potential Pitfalls of Exporting

8. False   Yes, it is false to assume that exporting is a "hunch" activity. On the contrary, exporting has guidelines that should be followed to aid managers in the exporting process.
    Difficulty: hard
    Topic: Designing an Export Strategy

9. True   Yes, the International Trade Administration (ITA) offers excellent export counseling to companies.
    Difficulty: easy
    Topic: Designing an Export Strategy

10. False   Yes, the import process basically mirrors the export process.
    Difficulty: moderate
    Topic: Import Strategy

11. True   Yes an export may go directly to a customer or may first go to an intermediary.
    Difficulty: moderate
    Topic: Third-Party Intermediaries

12. True   Yes, freight forwarders are used for both imports and exports, as one company's exports are another company's imports.
   Difficulty: moderate
   Topic: Foreign Freight Forwarders

13. False   Although all export licenses need to be carefully documented, there are two types of export licenses; one is a general license and the other the more restrictive individually validated license.
   Difficulty: hard
   Topic: Documentation

14. False   Yes, it is false to assume that all letters of credit are irrevocable, as this condition is part of the negotiating process between buyer and seller.
   Difficulty: hard
   Topic: Methods of Payment

15. True   Yes, in a countertrade arrangement a number of stakeholders may be involved.
   Difficulty: hard
   Topic: Countertrade

Multiple Choice

1. c.   Yes, this is not a recommendation by Grieve's president Calabrese. Instead, he recommended working hard and focusing on the business objectives instead of spending too much time on sightseeing and play.
   Difficulty: hard
   Topic: Case: Grieve Corporation: A Small Business Export Strategy

2. b.   Yes, these factors drive a company's decision process regarding entry modes.
   Difficulty: hard
   Topic: Export Strategy

3. c.   Yes, although small companies with appropriate market niches may have a high volume in exports, the general findings show that large companies must export to maintain high sales volume.
   Difficulty: hard
   Topic: Characteristics of Exporters

4. d.   Yes, this is a strategy a company should undertake and is not considered a potential pitfall of exporting.
   Difficulty: hard
   Topic: Potential Pitfalls of Exporting

5. b.   Yes, U.S. companies may obtain current statistics on exports from these organizations.
   Difficulty: moderate
   Topic: Designing an Export Strategy

6. a.   Yes, the first segment of imports is customer driven, whereas the second segment is driven by the importing company's strategic needs.
   Difficulty: moderate
   Topic: Import Strategy

7. b.   This is a critical area and should be considered before the goods are imported because tariff classifications tend to be nebulous and can add considerably to the cost of imports.
   Difficulty: moderate
   Topic: The Role of Customs Agents

8.   c.   Yes, good improperly marked as to their country of origin could be penalized with fines and or additional import duties.

               Difficulty: hard
               Topic: Import Strategy

9.   b.   Yes, the purpose of the drawback provision is to allow domestic manufacturers to add foreign-made components to domestically produced goods in order to export these goods without being penalized with import duties on these components.

               Difficulty: hard
               Topic: The Role of Customs Agents

10.   d.   Yes freight forwarders are intermediaries who offer their expertise in moving goods from one location to another and may provide additional services such as packing, crating, insurance, and selecting the most appropriate mode of transportation for a particular type of goods.

               Difficulty: hard
               Topic: Third-Party Intermediaries

11.   a.   Yes, sales representatives tend to facilitate the push process in selling to distributors, to retailers, or directly to customers and do not become tangible stakeholders.

               Difficulty: easy
               Topic: Direct Selling

12.   c.   Although trading companies is not totally accurate in all cases, the above names generally refer to trading companies in Japan and Korea. The zaibatzu has been incorporated into the terms keiretsu and sogo shosha since WWII.

               Difficulty: easy
               Topic: Non-U.S. Trading Companies

13.   c.   Yes, the bill of lading is a primary and vital document of a trade transaction.

               Difficulty: hard
               Topic: Documentation

14.   b.   Yes, an irrevocable letter of credit cannot be canceled or changed in any way without the consent of all parties to the transaction.

               Difficulty: moderate
               Topic: Methods of Payment

15.   a.   No, the term offset refers to agreements by which the exporter helps the importer earn foreign exchange or the transfer of technology or production to the importing country.

               Difficulty: easy
               Topic: Countertrade

Chapter 18

Global Manufacturing and Supply Chain Management

CHAPTER OBJECTIVES

1. To describe different dimensions of global manufacturing strategy.

2. To examine the elements of global supply chain management.

3. To show how quality affects the global supply chain.

4. To illustrate how supplier networks function.

5. To explain how inventory management is a key dimension of the global supply chain.

6. To present different alternatives for transporting products along the supply chain from suppliers to customers.

TRUE/FALSE

1. Samsonite centralized its supply chain in a centralized European warehouse.

    Hint   Samsonite wanted to reduce reliance on wholesalers.

2. Samsonite chose not to participate in the ISO 9002 certification because Samsonite is a U.S. company, not a European company.

    Hint   The ISO 9002 certification demonstrates how companies implement quality in their operations.

3. Samsonite kept all R&D facilities in the United States.

    Hint   Samsonite needed to understand the European consumer preferences.

4. Suppliers can be part of the manufacturer's organizational structure or be independent of the company.

    Hint   Vertically integrated companies may be their own suppliers.

5. The output from a manufacturer may be shipped to a number of destinations.

    Hint   Manufacturers have a number of distribution options.

6. A manufacturer's output must be sold domestically.

    Hint   Manufacturers produce for many markets.

7. Supply chain management and materials management are closely related.

    Hint   The difference between supply chain management and materials management is one of degree.

8. Direct manufacturing is used by both Samsonite and Nike.

    Hint   Direct manufacturing or virtual manufacturing are strategic decisions undertaken by companies to suit their product line and manufacturing processes.

9. MNEs establish manufacturing facilities in Asia, Mexico, and Eastern Europe mainly to minimize labor costs.

   Hint Cost-minimization strategies force MNEs to produce in low-cost labor regions.

10. An important type of offshore manufacturing for U.S. companies is Mexico's maquiladora operations.

    Hint Offshore manufacturing takes place outside of a company's home country.

11. U.S. companies tended to focus on minimum defects rather than zero defects.

    Hint Compare the U.S. AQL to the Japanese TQM.

12. ISO 9000 is a concept started in Switzerland and now is a quality standard reserved for EU companies only.

    Hint ISO 9000 certification has been adopted by 90 countries.

13. Japanese companies tend to source raw materials internally rather than externally.

    Hint Japan is poor in natural resources such as oil and minerals.

14. Toyota's Production System emphasized price low price over quality.

    Hint Toyota has rigid specifications.

15. Foreign trade zones (FTZs) are areas in which domestic and imported merchandise can be stored, inspected, and manufactured free from formal customs procedures.

    Hint FTZs are a type of free holding area for manufacturing.

MULTIPLE CHOICE

1. An example of virtual manufacturing in international business is:

   Hint Virtual manufacturing is a strategy companies like Nike and Mattel use.

   a. vertical integration.
   b. horizontal integration.
   c. production on a company's premises.
   d. a strategy whereby manufacturing is subcontracted out to other companies.

2. The basic manufacturing approaches MNEs use include:

   Hint Consider a company's strategic marketing strategy.

   a. the centralized, regional, and multidomestic approaches.
   b. licensing, subcontracting, and multidomestic.
   c. MNEs only use the centralized approach.
   d. decentralized and subcontracting.

3. General Motors chose _____ as its first major plant location in Asia because of a good labor climate and economic growth potential, reliable infrastructure, and good access to auto suppliers.

    Hint   Selecting the number of plants and their location depends on many factors such infrastructure, location, and national image.

    a.   Philippines
    b.   Cambodia
    c.   Thailand
    d.   Vietnam

4. Plant layouts for production are different for Toyota in Japan than for their plant in Thailand mainly because:

    Hint   Cost of production dictates plant layout.

    a.   local codes require different construction.
    b.   Toyota plant layouts and production processes are consistent in all countries.
    c.   in Japan the plants are highly automated and in Thailand the assembly process is highly labor intensive because of differences in labor rates in each country.
    d.   the Thai plant is newer and therefore more automated.

5. The key factor to making a global information system work is:

    Hint   Consider what drives decision making.

    a.   a high-tech computer system.
    b.   information.
    c.   data.
    d.   the operator.

6. A major reason why U.S. companies that operate in Europe are becoming ISO-certified is to:

    Hint   ISO certification is a stamp of approval.

    a.   maintain access to the European market.
    b.   sell European produced products back to the United States.
    c.   serve the global market.
    d.   U.S. companies that operate in Europe collectively have opted not to be ISO 9000 certified.

7. The three major configurations for sourcing are:

    Hint   Sourcing may occur within a company or with outsiders.

    a.   vertical integration, arm's-length purchases, and keiretsu type of relationships.
    b.   horizontal integration and outsourcing are the only options.
    c.   vertical integration, arm's-length purchases, and outsourcing.
    d.   Both (b) and (c) are correct.

8.   _____are areas in which domestic and imported merchandise can be stored, inspected, and manufactured free from formal customs procedures until they leave.

   Hint   These areas have become popular as an intermediate step in the process between import and final use.

   a.   Shipping yards
   b.   Factories
   c.   Foreign trade zones (FTZs)
   d.   Airports

9.   Denso's kanban system was first implemented by Toyota in order to:

   Hint   Kanban is used in the Toyota City plant.

   a.   create a stress-reducing environment through tree planting.
   b.   create an orderly JIT system.
   c.   computerize the ordering process.
   d.   stop the formation of labor unions.

10.   Sourcing in the home country lets companies avoid numerous problems that include:

   Hint   Consider home-country advantages and foreign disadvantages.

   a.   labor strife, language differences, and foreign exchange rates.
   b.   language differences, weather changes, and cultural differences.
   c.   There are few differences between sourcing from a home country of a foreign country.
   d.   language differences, culture, currency, and tariffs.

INTERNET EXERCISES

Exercise 1.
Samsonite Europe
http://www.samsonite-europe.com/
Explore the company information, shop and dealer locator, and product catalogue. Briefly describe how this Web site relates to the Samsonite case and the supply chain management concept.

Exercise 2.Nike
http://Saigon.com/~nike/ and   http://cbae.nmsu.edu/~dboje/nike.html
Compare the content within these Web sites. Then discuss the ethical issues Nike is confronted with in its effort to use subcontractors.

Exercise 3.
TQM Sources
http://www.ferris.edu/htmls/connect/TQM/ELSEWHER.HTM
Double click on three to four TQM BBS files of your choice. Discuss your findings and how these relate to TQM issues around the world.

Exercise 4.
ISO 9000
http://www.connect.ab.ca/~praxiom/ and http://fox.nstn.ca/~cottier/overview/ISO_9000/iso.html Study the content in each Web site and describe the ISO 9000 plus concept and relate it to international business and global manufacturing. Consider the costs and the benefits to MNEs and to consumers.

Exercise 5.
Council of Logistics Management
http://www.clm1.org/index.asp
Click on several links including: Our Mission, Membership, Resources, Publications. Discuss if this Web site is a useful tool for MNEs. Why or why not?

CHAPTER 18 ANSWER KEY

True/False

1. **True**   Yes, once Samsonite had established a strong European market, the company invested heavily in information technology to link retailers to its warehouse, which allowed for a more effective European distribution system.
   Difficulty: moderate
   Topic: Case: Samsonite's Global Supply Chain

2. **False**   Samsonite became ISO 9002 certified and also GS Mark certified, which is the #1 government regulated product test in Germany.
   Difficulty: hard
   Topic: Case: Samsonite's Global Supply Chain

3. **False**   Samsonite expanded R&D facilities to an additional site in Europe once the European business grew.
   Difficulty: moderate
   Topic: Case: Samsonite's Global Supply Chain

4. **True**   Yes, the above statement shows that suppliers may be internal to the company or external.
   Difficulty: hard
   Topic: Introduction

5. **True**   Yes, manufacturers may ship to other intermediaries or ship directly to the customer.
   Difficulty: moderate
   Topic: Introduction

6. **False**   A manufacturer's products go where the demand and the marketing strategy for the product are. It is not correct to assume that only a domestic market can be served.
   Difficulty: easy
   Topic: Introduction

7. **True**   Materials management focuses on transportation and storage of materials and goods, and supply chain management extends to suppliers and customer relations, but they are part of the same process.
   Difficulty: moderate
   Topic: Introduction

8. **False**   Samsonite established its own manufacturing facilities near its markets in Europe, whereas Nike uses subcontractors who have their own factories in areas such as China.
   Difficulty: moderate
   Topic: Global Manufacturing Strategies

9. **True**   Although MNEs may also establish manufacturing facilities in the above area to serve local customers, the major reason for locating in these regions is to minimize labor costs.
   Difficulty: easy
   Topic: Manufacturing Compatibility

10. **True**   Yes, the benefits of establishing a maquiladora are especially attractive to companies for which 30% or more of the product cost is labor.
    Difficulty: moderate
    Topic: Manufacturing Compatibility

11. **True**   Yes, U.S. companies tended to operate on the acceptable quality level (AQL) that allowed an acceptable level of bad quality.
    Difficulty: moderate
    Topic: Quality

12. False   ISO 9000 is a set of five universal standards for a Quality Assurance system that is accepted around the world.
Difficulty: moderate
Topic: Quality Standards

13. False   Yes, it is false to assume that Japan can rely on its own natural resources to supply its domestic industries.
Difficulty: hard
Topic: Supplier Networks

14. False   Toyota observes how manufacturers organize their factories and make its parts and expects high quality as well as annual price reductions and on-time deliveries.
Difficulty: moderate
Topic: Supplier Relations

15. True   Yes, FTZs are free from formal customs procedures until the goods leave the zones.
Difficulty: moderate
Topic: Foreign Trade Zones

Multiple Choice

1. d.   Yes, virtual manufacturing refers to a company subcontracting production to outside manufacturers.
Difficulty: hard
Topic: Global Manufacturing Strategies

2. a.   Yes the centralized approach tends to be the home-country initial approach that is followed by a regional approach such as Samsonite's location in Europe to be followed by locations in specific countries where local markets are lucrative.
Difficulty: moderate
Topic: Manufacturing Configuration

3. c.   Yes, GM had also considered the Philippines, but Thailand met many of GM's location requirements.
Difficulty: moderate
Topic: Plant Location Strategies

4. c.   Yes, work processes are designed to reflect the most cost-effective layout for local conditions.
Difficulty: hard
Topic: Layout Planning Strategies

5. b.   Yes, although this may seem obvious, it must be noted that information may be obtained from many sources including people and technology.
Difficulty: hard
Topic: Global Supply Chain Management

6. a.   ISO 9000 and plus certification is considered a prerequisite for purchase considerations by many Europeans, and some European companies will not do business with a supplier unless the supplier's supplier is also certified.
Difficulty: hard
Topic: Quality Standards

7. a.   Yes, companies may act as their own suppliers if they are vertically integrated, they may buy from outside suppliers, or they may buy from a consortium such as a keiretsu.
Difficulty: moderate
Topic: Supplier Networks

8.   c.   Yes, FTZs are zones intended to encourage companies to locate in the country by allowing them to defer duties, pay less duties, or avoid certain duties completely. FTZs tend to be located near ports of entry.

Difficulty: moderate

Topic: Foreign Trade Zones.

9.   b.   Yes, kanban literally means "card" or "visible record" and is used to control flow of production through a factory.

Difficulty: hard

Topic: Case: Denso Corporation and Global Supplier Relations

10.   d.   Yes, these are among a number of reasons why domestic sourcing can be simpler than sourcing from abroad.

Difficulty: easy

Topic: Supplier Networks

Chapter 19

Multinational Accounting and Tax Functions

CHAPTER OBJECTIVES

1. To examine the major factors influencing the development of accounting practices in different countries and the worldwide harmonization of accounting principles.

2. To explain how companies account for foreign-currency transactions and translate foreign-currency financial statements.

3. To describe the impact of accounting methods on the evaluation of foreign operations.

4. To investigate the U.S. taxation of foreign-source income.

5. To examine some of the major non-U.S. tax practices and to show how international tax treaties can alleviate some of the impact of double taxation.

TRUE/FALSE

1. German companies tend to be more conservative than U.S. companies in reporting earnings.

    Hint   The German legal system is highly codified and prescriptive.

2. U.S. accounting standards are oriented to the stock market, whereas German accounting gives preferences to the information needs of creditors and tax authorities.

    Hint   In the United States there is a focus on equity capital, but Germans rely more on banks as a source of funding.

3. German companies have a long history of being listed on the New York Stock exchange.

    Hint   The U.S. Securities and Exchange Commission requires stiff reporting requirements.

4. KPMG Deutsche Treuhandgesellaschaft audited the DaimlerChrysler financial statements that mixed U.S. and EU GAAP.

    Hint   The SEC allowed some flexibility in combining two GAAP systems.

5. Bringing together two accounting systems from two companies in two separate countries was relatively simple and straightforward.

    Hint   There are many hidden complexities in creating a new accounting system.

6. The role of the corporate controller has contracted in light of international activities.

    Hint   International business had added complexity to corporate financial analysts.

7. Managers need to determine who the key users are of their financial information in order to establish accounting objectives.

    Hint   Financial information should focus on user needs.

8. Colonial ties can be seen in accounting practices internationally.

   Hint   Former French colonies use the French model for accounting practices.

9. German companies tend to be very conservative in recording profits.

   Hint   German banks are concerned with liquidity.

10. Because accounting standards and practices differ significantly worldwide, it is impossible to classify them.

    Hint   Authors have used the concept of natural science to classify accounting systems in various countries.

11. The need to raise capital outside of their home-country capital markets is creating a force for global harmonization of accounting standards.

    Hint   Standardization for financial statements eases the capitalization process.

12. The EU has decided to oppose the International Accounting Standards Committee's efforts for harmonization of standards.

    Hint   The EU is playing a key role in creating reporting standards for its members.

13. The major challenge to the supremacy of ISAC GAAP is the United States.

    Hint   There are many differences between ISAC GAAP and U.S. GAAP.

14. U.S. MNEs keep financial statements from subsidiaries in foreign countries stated in the host-country's currencies to avoid confusion.

    Hint   Investors need to understand their worldwide activities.

15. Foreign exchange is not an issue for Coca-Cola because it operates globally.

    Hint   Coca-Cola writes an annual report on all of its holdings.

MULTIPLE CHOICE

1. When comparing U.S. accounting standards to German accounting standards, one could generalize by saying that:

   Hint   U.S. companies focus on equity capital and German companies rely on banks for capital.

   a. U.S. accounting practices are more conservative and German practices tend to be more transparent.
   b. U.S. accounting is focused on earnings and German accounting is focuses on asset valuation.
   c. both U.S. and German accounting practices are very similar.
   d. the United States uses an historic approach and the Germans use an asset valuation approach.

2. Taxation has a big influence on accounting standards and practices in Japan and France, but it is less important in:

Hint Tax laws influence reporting standards.

a. Germany.
b. All countries are highly influenced by taxation considerations.
c. the United States.
d. Switzerland.

3. With respect to accounting, secrecy and transparency indicate the degree to which companies:

Hint Secrecy tends to reveal little and transparency is open for scrutiny.

a. cheat on their taxes.
b. disclose information to the public.
c. manage their businesses.
d. trust their accounting departments.

4. Optimism and conservatism, in an accounting and not a political sense, are the degree of caution that companies exhibit in:

Hint Consider the different accounting practices of Germany and the U.S.

a. valuing assets and recognizing income.
b. using spreadsheets.
c. acquiring assets.
d. Both (b) and (c) are correct.

5. The major accounting influences on countries that fit into the macrouniform category are:

Hint Consider the meaning of macrouniform.

a. pragmatic business practices.
b. business economics theory.
c. Laissez-faire.
d. government economics, governmental, tax, and legal.

6. The International Accounting Standards Committee's (IASC) turning point in the significance of standards came:

Hint The IASC is comprised of 143 professional accounting organizations representing 104 countries and has worked towards harmonizing accounting standards since 1973.

a. when the International Organization of Securities Commissions (IOSCO) announced publicly that it would endorse IASC standards if the IASC developed a set core of standards acceptable to IOSCO.
b. when IOSCO accepted IASC recommendations as a standard.
c. when the U.S. Sec accepted IASC standards.
d. when Germany, the U.K., and the United States joined IASC.

7. Translation of foreign-currency financial statements is a two-step process in the United States that consists of:

Hint The process of restating foreign-currency statements into U.S. dollars is translation

a. translation into English and an audit by the IRS.
b. translate all foreign currency amounts into U.S. dollars and document this electronically.
c. converting foreign currency financial statements into statements consistent with U.S. GAAP and translating all foreign currency amounts into U.S. dollars.
d. This two-step process is no longer required.

8. To gain tax advantage from exporting, a U.S. company can set up a:

Hint To qualify, a company must be engaged in the exporting of either merchandise or services, such as engineering or architectural services.

a. foreign sales corporation (FSC).
b. mailbox company in another country.
c. a foreign corporation.
d. There are no tax advantages from exporting for U.S. companies.

9. Taxation of corporate income is accomplished through one of two approaches in most countries. The United States uses the:

Hint The two taxation approaches are: the separate entity approach and the integrated system approach.

a. separate entity approach.
b. integrated approach.
c. split-rate approach.
d. Both (b) and (c) are correct.

10. An MNE aiming to maximize its cash flow worldwide and minimize its taxes should concentrate profits in:

Hint Some countries have lower tax rates than others.

a. the home country.
b. gold bullion.
c. Germany.
d. low-tax/tax-haven countries.

INTERNET EXERCISES

Exercise 1.
DaimlerChrysler
http://www.daimlerchrysler.de/index_e.htm
Access both English and German (Deutsch) home pages and give both a comparative overview to get a sense of the complexities this newly formed company faces with their merger.
Then, access the English version home page and explore a number of links to include: Businesses, Board of Management, Worldwide Locations and DaimlerChrysler: One Company—One Vision.
Write a brief synopsis of your findings and relate this to the challenges regarding reporting functions that were discussed in Chapter 19.

Exercise 2.
FASB
http://www.Rutgers.edu/Accounting/raw/fasb/
Give a brief description of the board's main objectives.

Exercise 3.
IASC
http://www.Rutgers.edu/Accounting/raw/fasb/IASC/iascpg2d.htm
Compare IASC Standards and U.S. GAAP. Discuss your findings in a brief essay.

Exercise 4.
GAAP
http://www.Macmillan-reference.co.uk/EandF/gaap.htm and http://www.gaap.ru/">www.gaap.ru/</A
Compare the two Web sites regarding global issues on GAAP and discuss your findings in relation to the material in Chapter 19.

Exercise 5.
IOSCO
http://www.iosco.org/gen-info_01.html
Discuss their mission in relation to international accounting standards in a succinct essay.

CHAPTER 19 ANSWER KEY

True/False

1. True   Yes, there is a very strict accounting tradition in Germany that gives preference to the information needs of creditors and tax authorities.
    Difficulty: moderate
    Topic: Case: The Merger of Daimler-Benz and Chrysler—the Accounting Issues

2. True   Yes, U.S. accounting practices are oriented to the stock market, which means they are much more transparent than would be the case in Germany.
    Difficulty: hard
    Topic: Different Accounting Traditions

3. False   Daimler-Benz set a precedent by becoming the first German company to be listed on the New York Stock exchange.
    Difficulty: moderate
    Topic: The Merger

4. True   Yes, KMPG worked out a newly customized reporting system for DaimlerChrysler to suit the SEC reporting requirements.
    Difficulty: moderate
    Topic: The Merger

5. False   On the contrary, the process of merging a German and U.S. company was further complicated in trying to establish a new accounting system that would satisfy both countries' reporting requirements.
    Difficulty: easy
    Topic: The Merger

6. False   Rather than becoming simpler, the role of the controller has expanded beyond the traditional roles of management accounting in recent years because of the complexities of international considerations such as currency fluctuations, interest rate risks, tax planning, etc.
    Difficulty: easy
    Topic: Introduction

7. True   Although financial reports need to have correct factual information, the information should target specific users as well.
    Difficulty: moderate
    Topic: Accounting Objectives

8. True   Yes, there is a tendency to carry forward established accounting practices from colonial times.
    Difficulty: moderate
    Topic: Accounting Objectives

9. True   Yes, German companies tend to be very conservative in recording profits, which keeps them from paying taxes and declaring dividends while piling up cash reserves to service their bank debt.
    Difficulty: moderate
    Topic: Cultural Differences in Accounting

10. False   Although a simple and straightforward classification system for accounting worldwide is not yet available, it is possible to group various systems into categories that are determined by legal systems, government influence, and economic/business practices.
    Difficulty: hard
    Topic: Classification of Accounting Systems

11. True Yes, the present difficulty with diverse financial statements around the world is creating a force for harmonization in accounting standards.
   Difficulty: moderate
   Topic: Harmonization of Differences in Accounting Standards

12. False Rather than oppose the IASC, the EU chose to support the IASC so that it can also influence the standardization process rather than developing a competing standard.
   Difficulty: hard
   Topic: Harmonization of Differences in Accounting Standards

13. True The U.S. accounting standards dominate because the U.S. stock market is the largest in the world.
   Difficulty: hard
   Topic: Harmonization of Differences in Accounting Standards

14. False U.S. MNEs use a translation process to consolidate all foreign financial statements to conform so that investors can understand the worldwide operations.
   Difficulty: moderate
   Topic: Translation of Foreign-Currency Financial Statements

15. False On the contrary, by operating in over 200 countries and 50 functional currencies, Coca-Cola is directly impacted by exchange rates.
   Difficulty: easy
   Topic: Case: Coca-Cola and Its Global Challenges

Multiple Choice

1. b. Yes, this is a good generalization to show the different approaches to accounting in the United States and Germany.
   Difficulty: hard
   Topic: Case: The Merger of Daimler-Benz and Chrysler—the Accounting Issues

2. c. Yes, in the United States, accounting practices tend to focus on solvency and profit rather than taxation.
   Difficulty: moderate
   Topic: Accounting Objectives

3. b. Cultural and national differences in accounting practices tend to show degrees of secrecy and transparency among different countries.
   Difficulty: hard
   Topic: Cultural Differences in Accounting

4. a. Yes, optimistic countries tend to be more liberal in their recognitions of income, whereas conservative countries tend to understate assets and income.
   Difficulty: hard
   Topic: Cultural Differences in Accounting

5. d. Yes, these categories are represented in Sweden, Japan, and numerous continental European countries.
   Difficulty: hard
   Topic: Cultural Differences in Accounting

6. a. Yes, this supportive statement by IOSCO indicates that IASC is getting closer to harmonization of accounting standards.
   Difficulty: hard
   Topic: Harmonization of Differences in Accounting Standards

7.   c.   Yes, this describes the process necessary if U.S. or foreign companies want to list on a U.S. exchange.
     Difficulty: moderate
     Topic: Translation of Foreign-Currency Financial Statements

8.   a.   Yes, an FSC must maintain a foreign office, operate under foreign management, keep permanent records, conduct foreign economic activities, and be a foreign corporation.
     Difficulty: hard
     Topic: Taxation

9.   a.   Yes, also known as the classical approach, a company or individual is taxed when it earns income. A corporation is taxed on its earnings and stockholders are taxed on the distribution of earnings (dividends), and this tends to result in double taxation.
     Difficulty: hard
     Topic: Taxation

10. d.   Yes, countries such as Ireland can be both a manufacturing center and supply the EU with goods and is also considered a good tax-haven country because of its EU status.
     Difficulty: easy
     Topic: Planning the Tax Function

Chapter 20

Multinational Finance Function

CHAPTER OBJECTIVES

1. To describe the multinational finance function and how it fits in the MNE's organizational structure.

2. To show how companies can acquire outside funds for normal operations and expansion.

3. To discuss the major internal sources of funds available to the MNE and show how these funds are managed globally.

4. To explain how companies protect against the major financial risks of inflation and exchange-rate movements.

5. To highlight some of the financial aspects of the investment decision.

TRUE/FALSE

1. LSI Logic's Japanese subsidiary helped establish a line of credit in Japanese banks.

    Hint   The LSI Logic investment in Japan helped the company gain access to the Japanese capital market.

2. LSI did not participate in the Eurobond market because of the unattractive conditions there.

    Hint   The Eurobond market is for U.S. bonds issued in Europe.

3. The chief financial officer (CFO) plays a low-key role in an organization in spite of the rather grandiose title.

    Hint   The CFO functions are often divided into the controllership and treasury functions.

4. The CFO's job is less complex in a global environment than in the home environment.

    Hint   The global environment includes currency fluctuations and different laws.

5. Country-specific factors are a more important determinant of a company's capital structure than any other factor.

    Hint   Companies tend to follow the financing trends in their own countries and their own particular industry within their country.

6. One of the major causes of the Asian financial crisis was that Asian companies preferred equity capital to dept capital.

    Hint   Asia lacks a strong bond and equity market.

7. Subsidiaries may be able to obtain credit easier than local companies because they can enter into back-to-back loans when local interest rates are high.

    Hint   A back-to-back loan is one made between a company in country A with a subsidiary in country B and a bank in country B with a branch in country A.

8. Eurocurrency is any currency banked within Europe.

    Hint   Given the introduction of the euro as the new currency in Europe, the term Eurocurrency is now confusing.

9. Foreign bonds are bonds that are sold outside the borrower's country.

    Hint   The international bond market can be divided into foreign bonds, Eurobonds, and global bonds.

10. The international bond market is not a desirable place to borrow money.

    Hint   The international bond market allows a company diversity in its funding.

11. Offshore financial centers are located exclusively on islands.

    Hint   Offshore financial centers provide significant tax advantages to companies and individuals who do business there.

12. An important cash-management strategy is netting cash flow internationally.

    Hint   Netting means a company establishes one center to handle all internal cash/funds/financial transactions.

13. A company usually leads into and lags out of a strong currency.

    Hint   Lead strategies collect foreign currencies before due and lag strategies delay collecting foreign currencies.

14. When deciding to invest abroad, MNE managers must evaluate the cash flows from the local operations as well as the cash flow from the project to the parent.

    Hint   MNE assess opportunities and costs.

15. The secrecy possible in tax havens in countries such as the Cayman Islands makes them natural locations in which to hide cash that also makes this transaction automatically legal.

    Hint   Tax havens tend to shelter taxable earnings.

MULTIPLE CHOICE

1. Wilfred Corrigan of LSI Logic Corporation's international outreach concentrated on three key geographic areas that he called:

    Hint   LSI targeted Asia, Europe, and the United States.

    a.   the three sisters.
    b.   global triad strategy.
    c.   Eurasia strategy.
    d.   Both (a) and (b).

2. The four management activities related to cash flows are:

   Hint   The finance function in the firm focuses on cash flow.

   a.   capital structure, capital budgeting, hours of operation, and working capital management.
   b.   capital structure, capital budgeting, long-term financing, and working capital management.
   c.   working capital management, short-term financing, capital budgeting, and capital structure.
   d.   cash flow happens and is not managed.

3. Leveraging is often perceived as the most cost-effective route to capitalization, because:

   Hint   The degree to which companies use leverage—debt capital—varies from country to country.

   a.   dividends are tax deductible and interest paid to debtors is not.
   b.   interest tends to be low globally.
   c.   the interest companies pay on debt is a tax-deductible expense, whereas the dividends paid to investors are not.
   d.   Leveraging is not perceived as cost effective.

4. Eurocurrencies are different from Eurodollars in that:

   Hint   The term Euro is deceiving within the context of each total term.

   a.   Eurocurrencies are currencies banked outside its country of origin, and Eurodollars are dollars banked outside of the United States.
   b.   Eurocurrencies are currencies based in Europe and Eurodollars are dollars banked in Europe.
   c.   Eurocurrencies are also called euro and Eurodollars are dollars banked outside of the United States.
   d.   Eurocurrencies do not exist, but Eurodollars are U.S. dollars banked outside of the United States.

5. A major attraction of the Eurocurrency market is the difference in interest rates compared with those in:

   Hint   The Eurocurrency market is unregulated.

   a.   London.
   b.   Cayman Islands.
   c.   Eurocurrency interest rates are not the issue.
   d.   domestic markets.

6. A bond issue floated by a U.S. company in dollars in London, Luxembourg, and Switzerland is a:

   Hint   International band markets are divided into: foreign bonds, Eurobonds, and global bonds.

   a.   foreign bond.
   b.   global bond.
   c.   Eurobond.
   d.   Both (a) and (b) are correct.

7. U.S. companies first issued Eurobonds in 1963 as a means of:

   Hint   Eurobonds pay interest annually, are held in bearer form, and are traded over the counter (OTC) most frequently in London.

   a.   paying dividends.
   b.   avoiding U.S. tax and disclosure regulations.
   c.   raising significant chunks of capital because the bond denominations were in the $100,000 range.
   d.   U.S. companies have not been active in the Eurobond market until the late 1990s.

8. A change in the exchange rate can result in three different exposures of a company and they are:

    Hint   Currencies fluctuate often and both up and down.

    a.   translation exposure, transaction exposure, and economic exposure.
    b.   transparency exposure, transaction exposure, and economic exposure.
    c.   By forecasting exchange rates, MNEs avoid exchange rate exposure.
    d.   Currency fluctuations tend to favor MNEs.

9. When dealing with foreign customers, it is always safest for the company to denominate the transaction in:

    Hint   Use a currency that does not fluctuate.

    a.   Eurocurrency
    b.   the currency of the trading partner.
    c.   its own currency.
    d.   hard currency.

10. A key consideration for the future on securities trading is:

    Hint   Consider the changes that technology will bring to securities trading.

    a.   action from emerging nations.
    b.   regional economic integration.
    c.   securities trading will decline globally.
    d.   e-trading.

INTERNET EXERCISES

Exercise 1.
LSI Logic Company
http://www.lsilogic.com/
Read about this company and its investor relations. Relate your findings to the LSI case in Chapter 20. How has this company profile changed in relation to the information given in the case? How has the company remained the same? Be specific.

Exercise 2.
Financials.com
http://currencies.thefinancials.com/
Familiarize yourself with the Currency quotes section. Briefly describe your findings regarding Eurocurrencies and relate this information to the readings in Chapter 20.

Exercise 3.
Barra Equity Analytics
http://www.barra.com/
Consider the background information re. ADRs and the Global Equity Model. Briefly describe your findings and relate them to Chapter 20.

Exercise 4.
Cayman Islands, the Segoes, and Fiduciary Trust
http://www.destination.ky/gen/welcome.html
http://www.segoes.com.ky/sadmin.htm
http://www.fido.ky/
Explore the Currency/Banks link. Investigate offshore banking opportunities on the Cayman Islands. Also visit the Segoes and the Fiduciary Trust sites and write a brief overview of the offshore banking opportunities found at these Web sites. Relate this information to Chapter 20.

Exercise 5.
3M
http://www.3m.com/about3M/index.html
Go to the Investor Relations and 3M worldwide pages. Related the information on this site to the 3M case in the text and consider the complexities this company faces in the global arena. Consider the global challenges of companies such as 3M and summarize this within the context of the text and international business in general.

CHAPTER 20 ANSWER KEY

True/False

1. True   Yes, although LSI retained 70% interest in the Japanese subsidiary, the Japanese subsidiary helped the company gain access to Japanese capital with a 3% lower interest rate than in the United States.
   Difficulty: easy
   Topic: Case: LSI Logic Corp.

2. False   LSI was indeed attracted to the Eurobond market because it offered lower interest rates and quicker processing.
   Difficulty: hard
   Topic: Case: LSI Logic Corp.

3. False   The CFO role tends be more important rather than less important today because of the new complexities in domestic and international finance.
   Difficulty: moderate
   Topic: Case: LSI Logic Corp.

4. False   It is false to think that global environments are easier to manage than domestic environments.
   Difficulty: easy
   Topic: Case: LSI Logic Corp.

5. True   Yes, for example, Japanese companies are more likely to follow the capital structure of other Japanese companies than they are U.S. or European companies.
   Difficulty: moderate
   Topic: Introduction

6. False   On the contrary, Asian preferred debt capital to fund their growth.
   Difficulty: hard
   Topic: Global Debt Markets

7. True   Yes, back-to-back loans can be an advantage when possible and may provide a lower interest rate in some cases as well.
   Difficulty: moderate
   Topic: Global Debt Markets

8. False   Eurocurrencies could be dollars or yen in London or euro in the Bahamas, for example.
   Difficulty: hard
   Topic: Eurocurrencies

9. True   Yes, foreign bonds are sold outside a borrower's country but are denominated in the currency of the country of issue.
   Difficulty: moderate
   Topic: International Bonds: Foreign, Euro, and Global

10. False   Although not all companies are interested in global bonds, there are a number of advantages in this bond market over the domestic bond market.
   Difficulty: moderate
   Topic: International Bonds: Foreign, Euro, and Global

11. False   Offshore banking in this case means banking in a foreign country; some popular centers are Bahrain, London, and Switzerland.
   Difficulty: easy
   Topic: Offshore Financial Centers

12.   True   Yes, for example, an MNE with operations in four European countries could have several different intercompany cash transfers resulting from loans, the sale of goods, licensing agreements, etc.
        Difficulty: hard
        Topic: Multilateral Netting

13.   True   Yes, lead and lag strategies if carefully orchestrated can protect cash flows among related entities such as a parent and subsidiary.
        Difficulty: hard
        Topic: Formulating Hedging Strategies

14.   True   Yes, the former allows managers to determine how the project stacks up with other opportunities in the foreign country and the latter allows management to compare projects from different countries.
        Difficulty: moderate
        Topic: Summary

15.   False   Although much of the money sheltered in a tax haven is illegally avoiding taxes, there is some that is deposited there legally and to take advantage of a lower tax rate.
        Difficulty: moderate
        Topic: Ethical Dilemmas and Social Responsibility

Multiple Choice

1.   b.   Yes, this strategy considered the three major target markets for LSI products.
        Difficulty: moderate easy hard
        Topic: Case: LSI Logic Corporation and Global Capital Markets

2.   b.   Yes, these are the four major management activities related to cash flow.
        Difficulty: hard
        Topic: The Finance and Treasury Functions in the Internalization Process

3.   c.   Yes, these are the main reasons why many companies prefer debt to equity capital.
        Difficulty: hard
        Topic: Global Debt Markets

4.   a.   Yes, this describes the difference between these currency categories.
        Difficulty: moderate
        Topic: Eurocurrencies

5.   d.   Yes, a prime reason why borrowers are attracted to the Eurocurrency markets is that there may be a wide range and an attractive monetary incentive for borrowing Eurocurrencies over the domestic currency.
        Difficulty: hard
        Topic: Eurocurrencies

6.   c.   Yes, this describes a Eurobond in that it is sold in countries other than the one in whose currency the bond is denominated.
        Difficulty: moderate
        Topic: International Bonds: Foreign, Euro, and Global

7.   b.   Yes, these reasons reflect why U.S. companies first issued Eurobonds.
        Difficulty: hard
        Topic: International Bonds: Foreign, Euro, and Global

8. a. Most MNEs will see all three types of exposure and must forecast the degree of exposure in each major currency in which it operates.
   Difficulty: moderate easy hard
   Topic: Exposure-Management Strategy

9. c. Yes, by negotiating the transaction to be paid in one's own currency, there is no risk regarding currency fluctuations for the seller.
   Difficulty: moderate
   Topic: Formulating Hedging Strategies

10. d. Yes, electronic securities trading is a key issue to monitor with regard to potentially significant changes in securities trading in the future.
    Difficulty: moderate
    Topic: Looking to the Future

Chapter 21

Human Resource Management

CHAPTER OBJECTIVES

1. To illustrate the importance of human resources in international business relations.

2. To explain the unique qualifications of international managers.

3. To evaluate issues that arise when companies transfer managers abroad.

4. To examine companies' alternatives for recruitment, selection, compensation, and development of international managers.

5. To discuss how national labor markets can affect companies; optimum methods of production.

6. To describe country differences in labor policies and practices.

7. To highlight international pressures on MNEs' relations with labor worldwide.

8. To examine the effect of international operations on collective bargaining.

TRUE/FALSE

1. Peter Drucker believes that a truly multinational company must employ managers who have an international perspective "in a world in which national passions are as strong as ever."

   Hint   Peter F. Drucker believes a geocentric orientation for multinational managers.

2. Dow's strategy to send some of the best people abroad so that everyone will want them when they come back was an attempt to show employees that foreign assignments would be beneficial to their career.

   Hint   Dow's employees were reluctant to take foreign assignments because of a fear that repatriation would result in unacceptable positions at home.

3. If company chooses to transfer a large segments of home country employees to a host country, the only real factor to consider is the compensation differential.

   Hint   Hiring expatriates of third-country nationals can have legal implications.

4. International companies realize that management practices and styles are universal.

   Hint   National culture and traditions tend to influence behavior and preferred management styles.

5. There is less need to impose standard human resource practices when a company has a multidomestic strategy.

   Hint   A multidomestic strategy differentiates and customizes.

6. Communications can be eased in non-English-speaking countries if headquarters and subsidiary management simply use English as the common language.

   Hint   The international language of business is English.

7. Feeling-type managers are apt to be more effective in cross-border integration than thinking-type managers.

   Hint   Feeling-type managers are concerned with how decisions will affect others.

8. In a transnational strategy, the company adapts to the local way of operating.

   Hint   Transnational companies tend to transfer the best policies and practices regardless of where they originate.

9. Among Europeans, Germans and Italians enjoy taking foreign assignments most.

   Hint   Germans and Italians value family life that also includes extended family members.

10. It is estimated that U.S. companies may spend close to $1 million to finance an expatriate's three-year foreign assignment.

    Hint   A Western lifestyle can be costly in many foreign countries.

11. One of the critical adaptive skills for expatriate success when entering a new culture is the ability to perceive correctly what is occurring within the host society.

    Hint   Adjusting to a new situation requires awareness of a situation.

12. The amount and type of compensation is consistent for employees throughout an organization regardless of where they are relocated.

    Hint   Living conditions and cost-of-living expenses vary.

13. Labor and management tend to view each other in very similar ways all around the globe.

    Hint   Labor management interactions are built on historical, cultural, and legal precedents.

14. Codetermination is a popular process in which labor participates in the management of companies.

    Hint   Codetermination is particularly popular in Northern Europe.

15. Labor unions are contained within national boundaries and therefore do not influence international labor issues.

    Hint   Consider organizations such as the ICFTU and the ILO.

MULTIPLE CHOICE

1. MNEs face numerous problems when moving workers internationally and in most cases use local labor unless:

   Hint   The MNE may introduce a new industry.

   a. home-country employees volunteer for a foreign assignment.
   b. there is a shortage of people with needed skills in the host country.
   c. local labor unionizes.
   d. it is more expensive.

2. Dow Chemical has been able to reduce the number of international trips that employees take by:

   Hint   Consider the new communications tools.

   a.   enforcing strict expense account audits.
   b.   increasing an employee's stay when on a foreign assignment.
   c.   the use of electronic communications such as e-mail and faxes.
   d.   Dow Chemical has increased the number of trips employees take to meet with other Dow Chemical employees.

3. MNEs using a multidomestic strategy will have _____ to transfer human resource competencies from one unit to another.

   Hint   Multidomestic strategies focus on the countries where the unit is conducting business.

   a.   large need
   b.   little need
   c.   continuing needs
   d.   no need

4. International personnel transfers between newly merged companies are important so that:

   Hint   Consider the cross-national merger between Daimler-Benz and Chrysler.

   a.   the two merged companies do not continue to operate like two separate companies.
   b.   the employees learn new stress management techniques.
   c.   newly merged companies do not encourage exchange of personnel.
   d.   None of the above is correct.

5. The three types of adaptive characteristics important for an expatriate to success are:

   Hint   Adaptation requires survival skills.

   a.   the ability for self-maintenance, flexibility and tolerance for the host-country environment, and having a supportive spouse.
   b.   the ability for self-maintenance including managing stress, the ability to establish satisfactory relationships in the host-country environment, and being fluent in the host-country language.
   c.   There are no specific characteristics that expatriates should have to adapt to a foreign environment.
   d.   the ability to maintain oneself including stress management skills, the ability to develop and establish satisfactory relationships in the host country, and possessing cognitive skills that help analyze and interpret the host society.

6. The four types of expatriate managers discussed in the text include:

   Hint   Expatriate managers have diverse personalities and needs.

   a.   free agent, heart-at-home, going home, and dual citizen.
   b.   free agent, heart-at-home, culture shock, and dual citizen.
   c.   free agent, heart-at-home, going native, and dual citizen.
   d.   The text does not differentiate between different types of managers, as expatriates tend to have similar personalities.

7. Workers' abilities and motivations vary widely; consequently, it is the _____ associated with labor that is important.

    Hint   Managers need to be aware of work ethics in the international labor pool.

    a.   compensation
    b.   benefits in additional to salary
    c.   output
    d.   happiness

8. When there is little mobility between social groups, a marked class difference exists that may add considerably to a company's:

    Hint   Class struggles between labor and management are difficult to resolve.

    a.   labor strife.
    b.   entertainment costs.
    c.   marketing costs.
    d.   Class differences do not impact business strategies.

9. In Japan unions are:

    Hint   In Japan, one union typically represents all workers in a given company and has only very loose affiliations with unions in other companies.

    a.   less militant than those in most other industrialized countries.
    b.   illegal.
    c.   highly militant.
    d.   organized as strong national unions.

10. Codetermination is a type of labor participation in a company's management and usually is intended to:

    Hint   Consider the meaning of codetermination as a collaborative tool.

    a.   establish an adversarial model.
    b.   cultivate a cooperative rather than an adversarial relationship between labor and management.
    c.   create a window to international labor organizations.
    d.   Codetermination is no longer practiced because it has been made illegal.

INTERNET EXERCISES

Exercise 1.
Dow Chemical Company
http://www.dow.com
Study Dow's Corporate Profile, Vision and History. Then, access the Careers at Dow page and explore their global career opportunities, careers brochure, and diversity brochure. Write a brief essay that discusses Dow's global recruitment strategy and career opportunities.

Exercise 2.
Microsoft
http://www.Microsoft.com/mscorp
Get a sense of this company's values and mission. Then click on the Jobs link and explore career opportunities with Microsoft in three countries of your choice. Consider Microsoft's recruitment and hiring practices from the information on this Web site. Does Microsoft have a polycentric, ethnocentric, or geocentric human resource policy? Discuss.

Exercise 3.

Microsoft

Hewlett-Packard

http://www.Microsoft.com/jobs/international.htm

http://www.jobs.hp.com/search.shtml

Compare the Microsoft job site with Hewlett-Packard's and consider how the companies differ in their recruitment strategies. Describe each approach. Hewlett-Packard actively recruits interns in various parts of the world. Consider why. Relate your findings to the readings in Chapter 21.

Exercise 4.

International Confederation of Free Trade Unions (ICFTU)

International Labour Organization (ILO)

http://www.icftu.org/

http://www.ilo.org/

Compare each organization's objectives. What is the purpose of each organization and how do they address international labor relations issues?

Exercise 5.

Towers Perrin

http://www.towers.com/towers/

Access their Global Reach page. Study their news page and access each regional area listed to find how this company operates in various parts of the globe. Then give an overview of this company's mission and how it fits with international human resource management.

CHAPTER 21 ANSWER KEY

True/False

1. **True**   Yes, Drucker believes international companies must overcome ethnocentrism.
   Difficulty: easy
   Topic: Dow's International Management Development

2. **True**   Yes, Dow uses a number of strategies to make foreign assignments attractive to employees and that is one of them.
   Difficulty: easy
   Topic: Case: Dow's International Management Development

3. **False**   In addition to cost factors, companies need to look at legal issues regarding work permits for foreign employees as well as a number of personality and psychological factors that may make a candidate unstable in a foreign location.
   Difficulty: moderate
   Topic: International Worker Mobility Problems

4. **False**   Although some international companies assume that management practices and styles are universal, most companies realize that management practices need to be adapted to suit the situation.
   Difficulty: moderate
   Topic: National Management Styles and Practice

5. **True**   Yes, companies tend to standardize less and differentiate more in a multidomestic strategy, and this includes the human resource management practices.
   Difficulty: easy
   Topic: Headquarters-Subsidiary Relationship

6. **True**   Yes, even non-English-speaking countries such as Italy and Saudi Arabia tend to communicate with each other in English.
   Difficulty: easy
   Topic: Headquarter-Subsidiary Relationships

7. **True**   Feelings-type people tend to be concerned with relationship building and cooperation that is necessary in cross-border integration.
   Difficulty: moderate
   Topic: Matching Style to Operations

8. **False**   Although a transnational strategy may adopt some local ways, it also adopts the best policies from other regions.
   Difficulty: moderate
   Topic: Matching Style to Operations

9. **False**   Although some Europeans such as Germans and Italians dislike moving to foreign assignments, other Europeans such as the British and Dutch are more willing to accept foreign assignments.
   Difficulty: moderate
   Topic: International Managerial Transfers

10. **True**   Yes, the National Foreign Trade Council estimates that U.S. firms typically spend between $600,000 to $1 million of a three-year expatriate assignment.
    Difficulty: moderate
    Topic: International Managerial Transfers

11. True   Yes, expatriates need good cognitive skills that aid in assessing what is occurring within the host society.
Difficulty: moderate
Topic: Some Individual Considerations for Transfers

12. False   Compensation packages tend to reflect local cost-of-living expenses and special needs such as education for dependents and housing allowances.
Difficulty: moderate
Topic: Expatriate Compensation

13. False   On the contrary, attitudes between labor and management may range from open and friendly to extreme hostility in various parts of the globe.
Difficulty: moderate
Topic: Comparative Labor Relations

14. True   Yes, codetermination has been mandated by legislation in a number of countries such as Germany.
Difficulty: hard
Topic: Codetermination

15. False   Yes, although there are labors unions that are contained within national boundaries, it is possible that they may gain support on certain issues from other labor unions outside of the country.
Difficulty: moderate
Topic: Assistance to Foreign Bargaining Units

Multiple Choice

1. b.   Yes, MNEs will hired from outside a host country if local people do not have the skills the MNE needs.
Difficulty: moderate
Topic: Introduction

2. c.   Yes, the new electronic communications tools offer MNEs a cheaper and faster way for employees to communicate with headquarters and various subsidiaries.
Difficulty: easy
Topic: Headquarters-Subsidiary Relationships

3. b.   Yes operations tend to work independently within each area.
Difficulty: hard
Topic: Matching Style to Operations

4. a.   Personnel need to become familiar with particular operating procedures of both companies so that the various international components of the newly merged company are better understood.
Difficulty: moderate
Topic: Reasons for Using Expatriates

5. d.   Yes, these are the most significant characteristics expatriates need to adapt to a foreign environment.
Difficulty: hard
Topic: Home-Country versus Third-Country Nationals

6. c.   Yes, these are the four types of expatriate managers the text discusses.
Difficulty: moderate
Topic: International Development of Mangers

7. c.   Yes, international managers need to consider a worker's output, which depends on work ethics, abilities, and motivation.
        Difficulty: hard
        Topic: Differing Costs of Benefits

8. a.   Yes, an undercurrent of antagonism between the working class and managerial class may manifest itself in labor unrest and collective bargaining.
        Difficulty: hard
        Topic: Comparative Labor Relations

9. a.   It is assumed that Japanese unions concentrate on one company and establish relationships within that company and therefore seldom strike. When they do have labor disputes, they may stop working for only a short period of time or may continue working while wearing symbolic armbands.
        Difficulty: hard
        Topic: Union Structure

10. b.   Yes, codetermination as a strategy is popular in many European countries and carries legal as well as social approval there.
        Difficulty: moderate
        Topic: Codetermination